A Guide to Successful Consulting

With Forms, Letters and Checklists

Steven C. Stryker

GOVERNMENT INSTITUTES

An imprint of

THE SCARECROW PRESS, INC.
Lanham • Toronto • Plymouth, UK

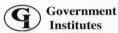 **Government Institutes**

Published by Government Institutes
An imprint of The Scarecrow Press, Inc.
A wholly owned subsidiary of The Rowman & Littlefield Publishing Group, Inc.
4501 Forbes Boulevard, Suite 200, Lanham, Maryland 20706
http://www.govinstpress.com

Estover Road, Plymouth PL6 7PY, United Kingdom

British Library Cataloguing in Publication Information Available

Library of Congress Cataloging-in-Publication Data
Stryker, Steven C.
  Guide to successful consulting : with forms, letters and checklists / Steven C. Stryker.
      p. cm.
  Includes bibliographical references and index.
  ISBN 978-1-60590-729-1 (cloth : alk. paper) — ISBN 978-1-60590-730-7 (ebook : alk.
paper)
  1. Consultants. I. Title.
  HD69.C6S86 2011
  001—dc23   2011039040

∞™ The paper used in this publication meets the minimum requirements of American
National Standard for Information Sciences—Permanence of Paper for Printed Library
Materials, ANSI/NISO Z39.48-1992.

Printed in the United States of America

Contents

List of Forms, Letters, and Checklists

Foreword

Many books treat consulting as a "get-rich-quick scheme." I cannot recommend any of them, because they do not support the true consultant.

Most only reinforce the negative stereotype of a consultant being someone between jobs. Consulting is more than just a job. It is a way of life.

Successful consultants understand this.

Steven Stryker has written a book that can help the novice understand the world of consulting. It is also valuable for the existing consultant as a guide to improving or formalizing an ongoing practice. This book is willing to go beyond the nuts and bolts and force the reader to consider some hard issues. Included are questions of ethics associated with providing services and understanding when it is both appropriate and necessary to turn down potential assignments. It raises the questions necessary to evaluate whether or not a career in consulting is feasible.

Good consultants are knowledgeable. Their consulting practice is based on extensive expertise in a given field. But more important, they are team players. Each assignment involves the transfer of knowledge to the client's staff. The best "work themselves out of a job," which is one of the most important attributes of the successful firm.

Consultants are enthusiastic and self-motivated. Their positive feelings and excitement spread through project teams. They listen well and ask questions to ensure understanding.

But consultants cannot generate miracles. To be successful in any engagement takes time and hard work. They also cannot be effective working in a vacuum. Consultants do not gather a few facts and then hide in a closet while the answer develops. Good consulting does not just happen.

As the founder of a major national association of consultants, I am glad to see the expanding interest in our industry. The numbers of consultants and their specializations are growing daily. The opportunities are there for the right people.

Each person must be realistic and recognize that consulting is not for everyone. However, if after reading this book, you feel that you have the ability, give it your best shot. Learn from the material presented in these pages. There is a hard-and-fast rule of small businesses: You can never plan on having a second chance. The ideas and procedures in this book will help you do it right the first time.

Good luck with your consulting.

—Steven Epner
Founder, Independent Computer Consultants Association

Preface

Today, there are more people practicing "consulting" than ever before.

These professionals work with various clients under various time, resource, and personal energy constraints to get the job done. Often, they are called in during a crisis, expected to perform miracles, and then to walk away leaving the executive to reap recognition and rewards. Few of these professional consultants are able to pause long enough to ask: What am I really doing, am I enjoying my work, and how can I improve my performance?

This book attempts to present a coherent picture of what is involved in becoming a reputable and successful consultant. Its tone reflects the pragmatism of many would-be or practicing consultants. That is, business people on the firing line do not have time to waste plowing through laborious texts. They want to learn and be able to apply their knowledge immediately. The information here is organized and presented in a readily usable fashion-from the idea of becoming a consultant to the notion of forming a consulting firm. For in each chapter the question of what a consultant does is answered: to solve someone else's problems in order to learn hew better to solve his or her own problems.

No book is complete without acknowledgments, and this one is no exception. Thanks go to Edwin Stromberg, Office of Policy Development and Research, U.S. Department of Housing and Urban Development, for his suggestions on federal contracting; Bruce Martin, Research Facilities Office, Library of Congress, for giving the space to be creative; Sandy Long, Social Science Division, Library of Congress, for a lot of well-timed assistance; Hubert Bermont, publisher of the Consultant's Library, for his support; Jacqueline Irwin, Administrative Assistant, College of Business and Public Management, University of the District of Columbia, for her serendipitous recommendation of Helen Hancock, Genova, Inc.—for her tireless effort in giving form to the book's substance; Barney Feinstein for taking enough interest in the project to suggest Susan Weiss—for her thorough, efficient, and wise editing of every page; my mother, Rick, Teri, and Deborah for their undying confidence in my abilities; and to Ted Jursek and Gloria Schafferof Prentice-Hall, Inc., who further completed my education about publishing while enhancing my reputation.

Whether you decide to begin consulting full-time either on your own or in a firm, part-time while still employed or after retirement, or in some other way, the important questions to ask yourself are these:

1. What services do you want to provide?
   * Quick and dirty advice
   * Ongoing, high-quality expertise
   * Project solutions
   * Services and/or products
2. To whom do you wish to provide these services?
   * Size of firm
   * Type of business
   * Stage of growth
   * Management style(s)
   * Contacts
3. How will you convince clients to use your skills and talents?
   * Personal rapport
   * Knowledge of their needs
   * Marketing initiative
   * Ways to respond effectively to change
   * Longer-term results
4. What business acumen do you need?
   * Set your consulting direction
   * Develop methods of providing service
   * Set up business practice
   * Ability to learn from mistakes
   * Evolve long-term business orientation

Each area is discussed herein in detail.

There are three constants that all consultants face each time they perform an assignment. They are fear of failure, ambiguity, and desire to perform. This book provides an additional way to deal with these constants along with experience. For although no book can substitute for experience, having a guide to excite more creative and productive ways of gaining experience can be an important link in building the bridge between practice and profession. For such ideas can enable you to integrate dollars and contracts, problems and abilities, and fun and humor.

Good luck and good times!

—Steven C. Stryker

Chapter One

So You Want to Be a Consultant?

SNAPSHOT

If you picked up this volume and are now reading these words, you are obviously interested in finding out what it means to be a consultant. Yet why this book1 There are other books and articles on' setting up a consultancy, on financial management, on consultant economics, and so on. But there are few books, if any, that discuss the wide range of consulting practices-from the solo practitioner to the large firm. This volume seeks to enlarge, enliven, and strengthen your knowledge, skills, and understanding of the business practices and services required to set up a successful consultancy. Each of the thirteen chapters includes an introductory section, entitled Snapshot; Sample Tasks, exercises based on the ideas or techniques discussed in the text; and Case Examples, real-life instances of consulting.

WHY CONSULT?

To begin with, what is consulting? In a recent book, Barbara Johnson defined the term succinctly: "A private consultant is a self-employed individual who, for a fee, gives experienced and skilled advice or service in a field of special knowledge or training." (Barbara L. Johnson, *Private Consulting: How to Turn Experience into Employment Dollars,* Englewood Cliffs, NJ: Prentice-Hall, Inc., 1982, Chap. One.) In addition, no matter what type of service the consultant provides, the consultant helps the client organization to cope with change.

Why does someone (yourself) consider becoming a consultant? Each case is different, but there are some common elements:

- Desire for a satisfying, long-term career
- Need for income because recently laid off, dismissed, or fired from a job
- Want some endeavor to net short-term gain because between career positions Lack of fulfillment in current position
- Interest in vocational life-style, which gives freedom to decide hours, income to be earned, people to work with, business direction(s), leisure activities, and place to live
- Opportunity to be a leader, advance the state of the art, build unique reputation, and enjoy a variety of challenges

Once you are aware of your motivations, you must know what skills are necessary for consulting. Here are the basic skills required to carry out any kind of consulting:

- Knack at finding and establishing new clients
- Facility in solving problems
- Ability to know what services you can provide, which ones you cannot, and which ones you would like to provide
- Ability to manage a small business

This book teaches you how to develop these skills. Understanding and applying them greatly increases your chances for success. Not understanding or misapplying them spells certain doom.

At this point, you might ask: "How is anything you have said thus far unique to a consultant or consulting in contrast, say, to any small business?"

There are differences, and the following personal traits distinguish consultants as a group:

Self-discipline. The willingness to motivate yourself to carry out the consulting engagement to the best of your ability and the contract.

Perseverance. The strength to complete assignments and to develop new business and services, all concurrently. In addition, the physical stamina to meet deadlines through long hours of work.

Patience. The calm to handle "16 things at once," to work under pressure, and to thrive on it.

Gregariousness. The drive to be outgoing, to establish rapport with clients, and to build ongoing relationships.

Adaptiveness. The flexibility to respond effectively to changing client situations and needs.

Confidence. The positive attitude to learn from and contribute to the client's organization while deriving enjoyment and knowledge from the experience.

Additionally, certain *qualifications* are necessary to practice consulting:

- Basic and extended levels of education. This includes a bachelor's degree with advanced courses, advanced degrees, and/or specialized training or certification.
- Some prior work experience in a business environment.
- Specific skills that have been applied to solve someone else's problems.
- Leadership skills.

In essence, the ideal consultant is someone who has worked, gained insight through success and failure, honed his or her abilities to the point where he or she can provide advice, and is encouraged to do so by family and friends.

Services make up the content of any consulting engagement. By definition, they are a combination of technical and behavioral elements.

Examples include:

- Planning or design
- Feasibility studies
- Options analysis
- Methods improvement
- Automation
- Training
- Technical evaluations
- Data collection/information analysis

Today, many individuals or firms offer consulting services. Does that mean that there is competition? No, because most services tend to be tailored to a specific client's requirements. Also, where clients ask more than one consultant to submit an approach to resolving a client concern, the responses tend to vary a great deal. Further, once you have established a reputation, you have also carved out a unique niche in the market. Thus the objective is to tailor your services to match your current or prospective clients' needs so that they will hire you.

To summarize, having the desire, skills, personality, qualifications, and services is primary to consulting. But the key element remains gaining and sustaining a client base. No amount of lucid information on paper can guarantee you success-this comes through your experience. The objective here is to provide a clearly marked road map to enable you to achieve success in your consulting "travels."

Chapter Two

Deciding to Be a Consultant

SNAPSHOT

When children are asked, "What do you want to be when you grow up?" they usually answer doctor, lawyer, policeman, fireman, nurse, teacher, mommy, or daddy. You rarely hear the word *consultant* because most children have never been exposed to consultants. Most adults decide to become consultants only after they have been exposed to and/or worked in another vocational area first. As we stated earlier, education, experience, and entrepreneurship are the prerequisites to independent consulting.

This chapter focuses on the decision to form an independent consulting practice. The key idea to keep in mind is that consulting remains outside the mainstream of business activities.

GOING OUT ON YOUR OWN

To begin with, let's assume that you are a software engineer in a medium size telecommunications firm, that you have gained a certain amount of knowledge that you use on the job, and that you would like to use more.

You also have contacts in the marketplace. In addition, you have an idea that you sense others might purchase. In addition, you are not satisfied within the organizational confines of your present company. Thus knowledge, contacts, ideas, and dissatisfaction are the reasons you begin to consider career alternatives.

MAKING THE RIGHT DECISION

Having reached this crossroad, **you** now need to analyze the positive and negative aspects of your current job situation. Exhibit 2-1 offers a way to do this. First, the aspects of consulting are evaluated; second, alternative choices are analyzed. From this dual examination emerges the personal and professional strengths and constraints of a consultancy. After completing this exercise, you can decide whether to begin providing consulting services.

Exhibits 2-2 through 2-5 illustrate how to complete Exhibit 2-1. In this example a seasoned business person with a computer background is deciding on her next career move. The consulting alternative provides her with the opportunity to act as an advisor using her experience, knowledge, and personality to deal with clients' needs. As a consultant she faces a greater financial risk than with the other three career alternatives, as well as working longer hours, making greater personal sacrifices, and having less job security. However, if successful, the consulting route could result in greater freedom, income, and professional and personal satisfaction than any previous position. Maturity, motivation, an understanding of the consulting process, and the ability to satisfy clients are required to create this success. These factors will assist you in deciding among the choices of Exhibit 2-4.

Sample Task 1

Complete Exhibit 2-1. Is consulting for you? If yes, what limitations must you face in becoming an independent consultant? If no, why not? Further, can your alternate career choices be incorporated in your consulting business? Finally, what steps must you now take to get started?

EXHIBIT 2-1

Framework for Deciding to Be a Consultant

1. List all the relevant factors to consider in becoming a consultant.
2. Based on your current situation, describe the advantages of each factor.
3. Think of several alternative career pathways.
4. Compare the consulting alternatives to these pathways.
5. Define and describe your consultancy,
6. Note the means to overcome the constraints and further the strengths of your consulting business.

EXHIBIT 2-2

Using the Decision Framework

Consulting Factor	*Advantages*	*Disadvantages*
Desire for greater independence	1. Maintain own schedule 2. Totally responsible for quality of consulting effort	1. Poor personality fit 2. Excessive work load or pressure could limit this independence
Desire to be your own boss	1. No bureaucracy to deal with 2. Can pick and choose consulting assignments	1. Have reputation to build 2. Job situation is uncertain, of high risk, with irregular Income
Enjoy solving client problems	1. Effectively respond to clients needs 2. Work for variety of clients in variety of situations	1. No prior consulting experience 2. Lack of client confidence
Enjoy providing thorough and long-lasting services	1. Major means of building reputation 2. Major means of increasing expertise	1. Long hours and excessive travel 2. Work on only one or few engagements at once
Enjoy making new contacts	1. Work closely with top executives 2. Contracting has tax advantages	1. Requires well- developed marketing and promotion methods 2. Need to develop client rapport prior to earning income
Understand accounting and ethical aspects of consulting and how to use accountant and lawyer	1. Ensures growth of consulting practice 2. Creates stability and long-term survival for consultancy	1. Comprehensive accounting and billing procedures needed 2. Become aware of when to turn down business and how not to give it away

| Need to define role and style of consulting | 1. Ability to be objective, outside client's situation, with skills to handle each
2. Seek client self- sufficiency | 1. Need to be astute listener and excellent communicator in many forms and contexts
2. Need to contribute new ideas that client will use
3. Need to overcome Stereotypes |

EXHIBIT 2-3

Career Pathways

1. Independent consultant	PriProvides advice to local computer stores as to which hardware/software packages are best suited to office automation, telecommunications, or teleconferencing.
2. Manufacturer's representative	Provides post-sales support to various computer stores in metropolitan area. This support includes primarily hardware demonstrations, marketing methods, installation of software, and upgrading of hardware/ software.
Franchise technical coordinator	Assesses the computer requirement at each computer store recommending which hardware to stock which soft ware to purchase and what supply orientation each store will have (a few lines with all models to a mix of lines with a few models for each line)
Software engineer	Works for small company to develop new software applications for sale to computer stores applications can be used on different computer hardware

EXHIBIT 2-4

Comparison of Career Choices

Pathway	Pro	Con
Independent consultant	1. Is own businessperson 2. Is involved with many different clients and applications of knowledge 3. Can lead to assignments with other types of clients	1. Has unsteady income 2. Is required to "beat the bushes" 3. Must work for minimum of several clients to make a decent income
Manufacturer's representative	1. Learns product line in depth 2. Has lots of contact with clients 3. Could lead to management position	1. Is required to travel frequently 2. Receives low salary; advances slowly 3. Needs to keep pace with technical advancements
Franchise technical coordinator	1. Keeps abreast of new computer products 2. Works as an internal consultant 3. Has much client contact	1. Has no career path 2. Doesn't make decisions, just recommendations 3. Is liaison between franchise and franchiser
Software engineer	1. Develops proficiency with software 2. Works as part of a team 3. Advancement is tied to company growth	1. Is under pressure to produce 2. Has little job security 3. Does technical development only

BEGINNING THE PRACTICE

Once you have made the choice to start consulting, your concerns are:

• How much consulting will I do at first?

EXHIBIT 2-5

Nature of Computer Consultancy

Purpose	To provide expertise on as-needed basis to retail clients with problems in applying their purchased computer software
Goals	To have an ongoing and responsive business to meet changing client needs
	To solve a specific client problem only once
	To develop a reputation for quality, rapport, excellence
Objectives	To obtain engagements from two clients in the next six months
	To fully capitalize the company for the $100,000 budget by the end of the year
	To have operational an active service promotion program for 1000 potential clients by next summer
	To package my expertise into salable items over the next year
Mission	To give advice in an honest and straightforward manner, paying particular attention to the results of such advice on the client as well as his or her customers, colleagues, and competitors
Things to do	Develop accounting and marketing and promotion schemes Research and contact potential clients Learn more about the skills of consulting Think through and evolve consulting style

---

- Where will I conduct business?
- What support services will I need?

To answer these questions, consider that few consultants go into consulting "cold turkey." Most consultants begin practicing on a part-time basis (while employed) to test their methods and services as well as build a client base. This period of transition can last a few months or several years. One problem that occurs during the transition period is shadow commitment. That is, the would-be consultant cannot provide full services with whatever energy is left over after job, family, and social concerns are taken care of. If more time could be given, additional assignments would probably follow.

Second, initially, most consultants work out of their homes or share rented offices. Whichever office space you choose, make sure that it is quiet, private, convenient, and spacious enough to contain vital equipment. Also, stock up on useful supplies. The adage here is: order what you need, but use what you order. Whenever possible, buy supplies at a discount.

Third, do not short-change yourself in using professional support services. To get started on the right road, invest some time and money in lawyers, accountants, graphic designers, insurance agents, computer analysts, secretaries, and so on. In addition, one of the best ways to better understand the fine points of consulting is to seek the advice of other consultants. If you plan first, work smart, and start smart, your consultancy will have a chance to prove itself before growing, rather than the other way around.

Case Example 2-1: Which Way to Turn?

Dave, a colleague of mine, worked **as** a career administrator for a medium-size company in the Midwest overseeing operations, purchasing, and compliance with government regulations. He had moved up the ranks slowly; this year marked his twentieth with the firm. But Dave was dissatisfied. As he said to me at lunch: "I feel as if the Peter Principle has worked on me in reverse. That is, as I have gained more responsibility, I have been less able to utilize it fully."

We talked a bit more and I discovered that Dave had been very active in local civic organizations. He served as program coordinator, publicity director, membership drive chairman, and he organized several conferences. "Do you want to stay with the company?" I asked. He answered that he would only if he could not find a better opportunity.

Together, we explored the possibility of consulting. "You could use your administrative, organizing, and human relation skills to assist local nonprofit groups in becoming more solvent," I suggested. "But what do I do for cash in the meantime?" he quickly retorted. "You might consider developing a marketing plan and making some initial visits to clients to ascertain whether there is a demand for your services and what services are in short supply. You could do this while you are employed. After discovering what you can provide and who would purchase such services, obtain an engagement with someone you know. Perform the consulting assignment, making note of your strong and weak points, then see whether and how to expand your consulting activities. The step-by-step approach is the most solvent. Oh-and I'm here to lend a hand and give you all the feedback you wish. Let me know how it goes."

Case Example 2-2: Can You Research and Free-Lance?

For about eight years Lenore Feingold worked as a researcher for a large pharmaceutical company in the Southeast. During this time, she concentrated solely on medical techniques to fight infection. She had produced five patients for her company and was one of the leading talents in antibody research. At a recent convention, Lenore was approached by a friend of one of her colleagues, Lynn Short. After discussing Lenore's work, Short said: "You have become one of the shining lights in infection research. Why don't you become a free agent? Put out information on your capabilities, achievements, and areas of interest; then submit these brochures to various laboratories, research and development centers, and universities. Work for the organization that offers you the best opportunity. During the engagement, circulate your brochure until another offer comes in. At the end of the current project, you will have several options to choose from. In this way, you can earn more money, work on the most exciting projects, and have a lot of autonomy and flexibility in your work. A reputation such as yours should be able to grow to the fullest. Would you be willing to consider this option?"

This example shows that the routes to a consulting career are as varied as the individual situation. Careful consideration of your own aspirations is the key to deciding on consultancy.

SUMMARY AND EXTENSION

Becoming an independent consultant requires both career and life-style changes. The first step is to assess your current situation: Is it challenging and rewarding enough for you in both the short and the long term? As shown, not everyone is suited to be a consultant; a combination of experience, expertise, contacts, and motivation is required. Knowing how to teach old dogs new tricks, what light to shed on problems, when to lead or assist the client, and the nature of your rewards are some of the daily tasks facing a consultant. Interpersonal skills are needed to engender trust and openness with the client. The ability to learn from mistakes is also important. The guiding principle for the consultant and his or her firm can be summed up in the proverb: Give me a fish and I will eat for today; teach me to fish and I will eat for the rest of my life.

Chapter Three

Opening the Practice

SNAPSHOT

Thus far we have discussed what consulting is about, who is likely to want to consult, who is likely to be able to consult, and what a consultant's activities might be. The next steps are to determine your consultancy's legal structure, develop a business plan, and discover the means for raising and using capital. These topics are described next. A word of caution: An independent consultancy is a small service business, and as such, faces the same risks as any other new business. Therefore, keep in mind throughout this chapter that mismanagement of consulting services, finances, or projects can lead to failure.

CHOOSING A LEGAL STRUCTURE

The form of your new firm depends on your assets, capital requirements, taxation considerations, and legal desires. One sound way to make a decision as to which form is best is to find a competent lawyer or accountant. Using the services of either an attorney or an accountant can prevent many undesirable situations and help expedite your success, Questions to help you discover the best legal structure for your firm and assess the competency and willingness of the lawyer or accountant to meet your needs are shown in Exhibit 3-1. (*Note:* An alternative to seeking private legal or financial counsel is to use the services provided by a professional association, Listed at the end of Chapter Nine. Any of these organizations can also be a source for discounts in health, life, or disability insurance.)

EXHIBIT 3-1

Questions for an attorney and an Accountant

Attorney	*Accountant*
What are the pros and cons of each legal entity given my situation?	What is the risk for each legal Entity?
What lows do I need to be aware of and why?	How wood I raise capital-now and in the future?
What are the procedures and costs of Starting each legal entity?	Which legal entity wood offer me the best tax status? Why?
Given my purpose today which legal entity wood serve me best why	What kinds of records should I keep and what type of planning is best for income tax purposes?
What kind of assistant do you provide in drawing up a contract obtaining liability insurance or representing me in case of law suits	Could you put me in touch with Commercial lenders? Will I be able to secure a loan? What kinds of profit structure should I have-profit, not for profit, or nonprofit? Why?
Are you available for question and Ongoing consultation?	Are you available for question and Ongoing consultation?

This section concentrates on presenting partial answers to some of the legal questions posed in Exhibit 3-1. A consultant can decide to organize a company in three ways: sole proprietorship, partnership, or corporation.

No legal documents are required to establish a proprietorship; you simply "hang out your shingle and do business.'" proprietorship exists as soon as there are business transactions. Although not required, many sole proprietors register the name of the consulting business with either the county or state government. This is done by printing the name and address of the consultancy, its owner, and the type of service in a local newspaper for a set period of time. Registration grants official status to the firm's operations. As a sole owner, you generally declare and pay your projected income tax in quarterly installments. Exhibit 3-2 lists the pros and cons of a proprietorship operation. As you can see, this kind of operation appeals to a consultant with few business assets who wants to be self-employed and reap the fruits of his or her labors

---

EXHIBIT 3-2

Characteristics of the Sole Proprietorship

Favorable Aspects

Easy to set up

Undivided profits

Responsive management/sole authority

Can sell firm at any time

Can change nature of business and capital structure without government approval

Tax structure advantages up to about $50,000 net

Constraining Aspects

Financially responsible for all business debts

Firm life limited by health and life of owner

Relative difficulty in obtaining long- term financing

Limited viewpoint and experience of owner

---

with a minimum of external encumbrances. As the business grows, thought can be given to incorporating. According to the 1977 U.S. Census of Service Industries, there are approximately 144,000 establishments listed under "management consultants and public relations firms." Of these establishments, more than 83 percent are sole proprietorships, with about 14 percent being corporations and 3 percent being partnerships. When the establishment assumes a pay roll (of which the U.S. Census says there are over 24,500), the percentage of corporations jumps to 75 percent, with sole proprietorships comprising 16 percent of the total and partnerships 9 percent.

These statistics confirm what is known throughout the business world- partnerships are the least common form of enterprise. Like the sole proprietorship, they are easy to put together, with no legal requirements a priori. However, it is highly recommended to draw up a written agreement to guarantee solvency (see Exhibit 3-3). In an active partnership, two or more people agree to participate in the operations of the firm. They share the profits, losses, management responsibilities, and debts incurred.

However, various people can act as legal or economic backers of the partnership without being actively involved in the firm. A *nominal* partner uses

---

EXHIBIT 3-3

Items for a Partnership Agreement

1. Date of formation of the partnership
2. Names and addresses of all partners
3. Nature of the business
4. Location of the business
5. Duration of the partnership
6. Type of partner and amount invested
7. Duties of each partner
8. Percentage of profits and losses shared by each partner
9. Limit on how much each partner can withdraw from the business
10. Statement of audit and financial control procedures
11. Provisions for one partner buying out another
12. Procedures for admitting new partners
13. Provision for dissolution and the sharing of assets
14. Settlement of disputes
15. Contingencies in case of absence or disability of any partner
16. Required and prohibited acts
17. Signatures of partners (notarizing is optional)

---

his or her name as a partner even though he or she has no direct involvement in the business. A *silent* partner does not take part in the operation of the business even though he or she may invest in it. These partners are *limited* partners in that their responsibility to the firm does not extend beyond the name or investment, respectively. As with a sole proprietorship, the firm name of a partnership should be registered.

Successful partnerships depend on the personal qualities of the partners, as illustrated in Exhibit 3-4. For a partnership consultancy to work, the skills and desires of all parties must be complementary. For example, one person can be an adept marketer, the other a capable analyst and writer. Or one person can market and consult in the education area; another can market and consult in the aerospace field. Yet they employ similar techniques in securing and carrying out contracts. Or both partners can act as a marketing team, and any subsequent contracts are managed by one of the partners. But the bulk of the "technical" work is done by analysts on an as-needed basis. Whatever arrangement evolves, keeping the partnership alive is another question altogether. No partnership is immune from disagreements, conflicts, or even court fights. Staying on top of a rapidly changing marketplace requires intense competition and causes internal pressures. Also, interests and motivation change as

---

EXHIBIT 3-4

Characteristics of a Partnership

Favorable Aspects	*Constraining Aspects*
Few startup costs	Partners personally responsible for all business debts
Sharing/pooling of management	Illness or death of general partner could cause dissolution
Divided responsibility for profits and debts	Potential conflicts over authority and control
Investor opportunities facilitated by range of partner arrangements	Relative difficulty obtaining large sums of capital
Tax structure advantageous up to about $50,000 net	Firm bound by the acts of any partner

---

new opportunities or attitudes emerge from prior consulting experiences. Keeping a partnership solvent means knowing how to satisfy the needs of all concerned in the long run.

Because of the risk in sustaining a partnership, many sole proprietors, adopt a "modified partnership" plan. Here each consultant retains his or her profit center; there is no formal agreement on sharing profits, losses, and liabilities. Instead, there is a sharing of resources-office space, facilities, and information. In this manner, if a project arises on which the consultants wish to collaborate, they can form a joint venture for the duration of the assignment. However, they are then free to pursue separate interests with no obligations to each other.

The third legal structure for a consulting firm, a corporation, is use when large profits are desired in an organizational framework. The corporation exists separately from any of the owners, officers, or directors. Its purpose is to allow for the orderly accrual of revenue and capital without the owners assuming personal responsibility for debts and liabilities (as is the case En a proprietorship or partnership). A word need be said here about financial obligations. With any of the three legal forms mentioned, if debts surmount income with no foreseen means of abatement, bankruptcy can be declared. However, a corporation can take a number of steps to prevent bankruptcy. In brief, a corporation is created as a separate legal entity from its owners. The owners are stockholders who purchase shares of stock in the corporation. A board of directors is elected by the owners to oversee the firm's operations.

EXHIBIT 3-5

Characteristics of a Corporation

Favorable Aspects	*Constraining Aspects*
Stockholders are responsible for amount of their investment	Activities of firm limited by charter and bylaws
Can rapidly transfer ownership	Extensive government regulations
Firm's existence is not dependent on any one or a few persons	Expensive to form
Can secure capital in large amounts through stock issuance	Numerous and sometimes excessive taxes
Company can draw on skills and experience of several competent Persons	Shared profits are received by stock holders only if dividends are Declared

---

The directors, in turn, choose officers who staff, organize, and control the business.

For a small consultancy, the owners, directors, and officers of a corporation may be the same. The owner-consultants own most, if not all, of the stock in the corporation. They then hire themselves as employees of the corporation. This way they can each draw a salary and be eligible for a range of employee benefits. Further, when properly structured, these benefits are deductible from the corporate taxes, not the employee/owner's taxes. As Exhibit 3-5 shows, the benefits of incorporating are the financial obligations and arrangements available versus the formation expense, public disclosure requirements, and taxation method.

Taxes can be a double bind for small corporations. Corporations are taxed on their profits and again on the dividends paid to stockholders. In 1958 the Internal Revenue Service introduced a Subchapter 5 type of corporate structure, which acts as a partnership in its tax assessment (see Exhibit 3-6 for requirements). Each owner is taxed on his or her share of corporate earnings. If a loss occurs, each stockholder may deduct such losses from his or her personal income tax. Further, such losses may be carried over from a previous year's taxable income.

In addition, since owner-managers are also employees of the corporation, they enjoy benefits in forming pension plans, securing group insurance,

---

EXHIBIT 3-6

Requirements for a Subchapter S Corporation

1. The corporation must be independently owned and managed and not a part of another corporation.
2. The corporation must be domestically based.
3. The corporation may have only one class of stock.
4. The corporation may have no more than 25 shareholders.
5. Only individuals or estates are permitted as shareholders; no corporations may own stock.
6. Corporate income or loss is reported by shareholders on their personal returns.
7. Nonresident aliens are excluded as shareholders.
8. All shareholders must agree on Subchapter S provision; otherwise, it cannot occur.
9. No more than 20 percent of revenue comes from dividends, rents, interest, royalties, or stock sales.
10. No more than 80 percent of revenue comes from foreign nations.

---

paying medical expenses, and remaining exempt from personal liability for business debts.

Forming either kind of corporation requires a license. To incorporate, a prospective consultancy must file with a state. Delaware is often chosen because of its tax advantages. It is mandatory that a name be reserved and verified for the corporation and a certificate of incorporation be prepared and submitted. As Exhibit 3-7 points out, a lawyer is sometimes needed to expedite this procedure effectively. Once the state approves the incorporation certificate, it becomes the corporate charter. A sample charter is shown in Exhibit 3-8. The charter, which announces the corporate intentions, is adopted by the owners at a meeting at which directors are also chosen. Such meetings must be held periodically and records kept of them.

Also, at the first meeting, the firm's bylaws are presented and voted on. Usually, these bylaws outline the means by which meetings are held, officers are chosen, directors are elected, stock and dividends are issued, the annual statement is prepared, and the bylaws are amended.

There are no hard-and-fast rules for when, if at all, a consulting firm should become a corporation. Generally, those consulting businesses with sufficient cash flow or personnel that are thinking of expanding to various cities or who require large facilities or machinery are ripe candidates for incorporation. A

EXHIBIT 3-7

Steps to Incorporation

1. Seek competent legal counsel.
2. Choose the state in which to incorporate.
3. Have incorporator(s) prepare a certificate of incorporation.
4. Apply to the state to incorporate.
5. Publicize application and name, and pay incorporation fee and franchise tax.
6. If the state official approves, a corporate charter is issued,
7. Secure proper licenses, tax identification number, and unemployment insurance account.
8. Hold stockholders' meeting to complete incorporation process. Elect board of directors and decide on stock and tax status. Approve bylaws.

Subchapter **S** arrangement allows the participants to raise working capital directly while avoiding an undue tax burden.

Sample Task I

As a new business owner, list the pros and cons for having a consulting firm. Now, which legal form is most suitable to your consulting practice? Why?

EXHIBIT 3-8

Elements of the Corporate Charter

1. Name of the company
2. Purpose(s) for which the corporation is being formed
3. Length of time for which the corporation is being formed
4. Names and addresses of the incorporators
5. Location of the principal office in the state of incorporation
6. Maximum amount and type of stock to be issued
7. Capital required at time of incorporation
8. Preemptive rights, if any, to be granted to stockholders and any restrictions on stock transfer
9. Internal organization and limitations on management decisions
10. Names and addresses of interim directors
11. Right to amend or repeal any article of the charter

Sample Task II

Draw up a plan for the expansion of your consultancy. What legal form would you have at first. Why? What events would cause you to change the legal form? Why? How would this change affect your ability to provide consulting services?

PLANNING THE STARTUP

Generally, after deciding the firm's legal structure, the next step is to secure the money required to begin operations. Most consulting firms need relatively little working capital to begin. But no consulting firm can hope to be successful without a business plan that:

- Defines the activities and goals of the consultancy
- Prepares a financial plan
- Charts a marketing strategy
- Provides a means of managing effectively

The plan is the firm's blueprint, illustrating the advantages and challenges faced by the consultant entrepreneur. It is the medium through which operational changes occur, major decisions are made, and control is exercised.

Exhibit 3-9 presents a sampling of the major items to be included in a business plan. Since the independent consultant's primary interest is to establish a client base, items7 through 9 of Exhibit 3-9 must be incorporated in a plan. Let's take a closer look.

EXHIBIT 3-9

Elements for a Consulting Business Plan

1. Purpose and rationale for the firm
2. Major services provided
3. Means of providing services
4. Financial requirements
5. Legal structure
6. Business operating philosophy
7. Assessment of the consulting industry
8. Alternative ways to build a client base
9. Contingencies

---

7. ***Assessment of the consulting industry.*** Determine the technological, economic, regulatory, social, and consumer influences on consulting. This can be accomplished through contact with other consultants, consulting firms, consulting associations, clients who have used consulting services, leaders in your area of expertise, statistical indicators from the U.S. Department of Commerce Census of Service Industries, articles in business journals, and so on.

8. ***Alternative ways to build a client base.*** Identify your primary and secondary clients, ways to provide services to them, and the short- and long-term results of your consulting business. Next, choose clients to approach initially (see Chapter Four).

9. ***Contingencies.*** No business is immune from the unknown. But preparing for the unforeseen can greatly assist you to stay profitable in case of sudden negative events. That is, what if you cannot meet your sales projections, you are unable to capitalize on new business, your largest client goes bankrupt, your offices are destroyed by fire, demand for your services increases fivefold in six months, you are sued far malpractice, and so on. Make a list of all the possible situations and ways to handle them; awareness can help dissipate any business shock or enhance any business opportunity that your consultancy might not otherwise sustain.

A basic statement outlining the goals, finances, and values of a consultancy is shown in Exhibit 3-10. This statement could be superseded by a charter or agreement, but it is still a good idea to draw up this type of plan, as it summarizes the major reasons for a firm's existence. Further, the plan for Syner-Think (Exhibit 3-10) is commonly used in securing debt capital from a bank.

EXHIBIT 3-10

Business Plan for Syner-Think

Principles
The firm of Saner-Think has a unique contribution to give to the consulting milieu. The perspective is based on the firm's ability to respond effectively to client engagements while evolving its own character. This viewpoint is unique in that it is the creation of the founders, whose vision for an integrated approach to consulting is found in all aspects of firm operations. The success of this firm will be measured by how sensitively

and appropriately the functions of planning, marketing, and controlling, and to a lesser degree, organizing and staffing, are executed. Efficiency and effectiveness are the watchwords. They assume greater meaning as the firm grows.

Provision of Services

The firm focuses on issues of energy management and energy conservation technology development. Specifically, the firm will provide policy tools and technology evaluation techniques to assist clients in the public and private sectors in meeting short-term objectives of energy and cost savings.

Securing and Executing Engagements

The owner-managers of this firm will use a vigorous marketing approach to obtaining new clients. Various issue areas will be defined and allocated to the partners. In turn, each will be responsible for a sales quota in that area. I Common marketing techniques will be decided on beforehand. The firm seeks to establish firm rapport with each client in order to develop a strong client/consultant relationship and resolve the client's issue in a timely and effective manner.

Cash Forecast

	Month 1		Month 2		Month 3	
Item	*Budget*	*Actual*	*Budget*	*Actual*	*Budget*	*Actual*
Revenue Past due income other income Total revenue						
Rent and utilities Telephone Photocopying						
Supplies Clerical help Automobile expense Equipment rental Other Total direct labor						

Business taxes Accounting/ legal fees Marketing Advertising and promo- tion Employee benefits Professional activities Total adminis- tration cost						
Computer time Clerical Reproduction Telephone Transporta- tion Per diem Miscellaneous Total direct expense Total costs Cash balance Desired cash balance						
Capital requirements Short term Longer term						

Ownership
The firm is wholly owned by its principals, who are its general partners. The Partnership Agreement specifies the obligations and responsibilities of the owners. Limited partners are not discouraged.

Operating Creed
This firm seeks to perform consulting services in a professional man- ner This means that each consultant must act in accordance with ethical

principles in fostering interaction and innovation in the client environment. Each assignment is accepted only with the understanding of producing timely and effective results within budget and on schedule. This plan
is to be made operational, to be reviewed periodically, and is subject to
change based on revised company goals and expectations.

Sample Task III

Define your consulting service. Develop five alternative means of increasing
your client base. Which one would you choose? Why? What contingencies do
you need to identify to help implement the chosen alternative?

Overall, the business plan gives substance, perspective, and direction to
your consultancy. Its effectiveness is measured in two ways: by how it is
formulated and by how it is used. The long-term success of the business
depends on revising and updating the plan in response to changing conditions externally and internally. (A further discussion on adapting to change
appears in Chapter Thirteen.)

As you know, data processing is one of the fastest growing industries in
the world. However, as shown below, new organizations sometimes cannot
grow at the same pace as the technology. A colleague of mine related the
following venture.

Case Example 3-1: The Cycle of the Oyster

In 1979, Julian Schwartz stopped working for a federal agency to go out on
his own. He had been involved in data gathering and analysis. At the suggestion of some colleagues, he decided to put together a few design tools for the
efficient entering and processing of information. Word got around about his
design tools, and quickly his skills were in high demand. So Schwartz began
consulting full-time. There was far more work than he could handle, so he
formed his own company to capture all the business he could.

The independent consultancy flourished with a lot of part time assistance
from others. In short order, the new consultant realized that he needed to
expand his firm by hiring full-time people. And this is where his problems
began. You see, Schwartz, the consultant, had a highly marketable product;
but he lacked the talented associates needed to increase his business volume.
The part-timers, in the main, were either permanently employed somewhere
else and "moonlighting" fox Schwartz or other consultants who wanted to
remain independent. Schwartz needed top-quality employees who could
solve problems. Although he made promises of sharing the wealth, getting in

on the ground floor and an open-door management style, he could not entice his associates to join him full-time.

Schwartz felt that without a cadre of full-timers the demand for his services could not be met, and thus his business would dry up. He finished the immediate contracts, yet with decreasing support from his colleagues. Finally, his business faltered.

Sample Task IV

Why do you think Schwartz couldn't make it? Any suggestions about what he could have done to reverse his situation?

FINDING INITIAL CAPITAL

The decision is not only how much money a fledgling consulting firm needs, but when it is needed and where it comes from. Given that capital is required to operate, there are primarily two kinds of money potentially available: equity capital and debt capital.

When the owner seeks persons or firms to become investors in the firm, the money invested is known as equity capital. The investor then becomes an owner or part-owner of the firm, depending on the amount of his or her contribution. However, the present owners are, a priori, under no obligation to ensure a return on the investors' capital or even to repay their initial investment. Yet, in practice, some type of assurance is given to the investor as to expected gain. That is,

- The cost of equity = expected earnings + investment, or
- The cost of equity capital = earnings per share + price per unit (of stock, bonds, secured, or convertible notes)

The owner and investor agree beforehand on the share of income from the investment. For example, if an investor puts up $10,000 for a 25 percent interest in the firm, and the projected annual revenue is $16,000, then

- Expected earnings = $16,000 × 0.25 = $4000.
- Cost of equity capital = ($16,000 × 0.25) + $10,000 or 40 percent.

That is, the investor expects a 40 percent return on his or her money. What happens if the investor does not achieve this? In practice, the investor assumes the risk, not the owner. If the consulting firm succeeds, the investor succeeds; if it fails, claims of all creditors are satisfied before those of the investor.

When the owner seeks persons or firms to lend money with an obligation for the owner to repay the loan with interest, the money lent is known as debt capital. Failure to meet the payment schedule could force the consultant into bankruptcy. The owner(s) assume all risk for the capital. This means that the lender has claim to the assets of the business if the consultant(s) do not repay the loan. But generally lender(s) have no say in how to run the business, in contrast to investors. To compute the effective cost of a lean, the owners use the following formula:[1]

cost of debt capital
= (interest rate) × (I − effective income tax bracket)
Thus, if the interest rate is 20 percent and your tax bracket is 40 percent,
cost of debt capital = 20% × (I − 40%) = 0.2 × 0.6 = 12%

That is, the true cost of borrowing (after taxes) is12 percent. Consequently, the owner(s)' cost for an equity investor is higher than for a lender a since the investor is taking the additional risk of obtaining no income from his or her investment.

Exhibit 3-11 lists the different characteristics of investors and lenders.

Investors are looking for a short-term, high return on their funds. This implies that a likely candidate for investment is a high-revenue growth firm or one that needs an additional infusion of capital to expand beyond its present successful size. Formal procedures are used to secure such funds from companies, and informal discussions are used with individuals. In fact, the formal procedure is similar to applying for a loan (see below). Informally, the owner and investor meet and talk over the firm's financial situation. If the potential investor is interested in the firm's activities, an investment could be forthcoming. If so, the transaction should be made in writing-spelling out the investor's new duties or responsibilities-and then notarized. This agreement is also part of the formal procedure for attracting corporate investors.

For a lender, 'the situation is qualitatively different. The consultant owner visits a lender to apply formally for a loan. The lender's major concern is not how much to lend, but the owner's ability to pay back the loan. This "ability" is ascertained in the manner shown in Exhibit 3-12. The cash forecast section of the business plan (Exhibit 3-70) highlights the business plan section of Exhibit 3-12. The procedure for obtaining a loan from commercial or government lenders is similar, yet a major difference is that government agencies loan money based on how well the applicant's request matches the agency's mandate. Personal factors and economic conditions are relatively unimportant-not so for the private bank, mortgage company, or other commercial lender.

---

[1]Different formulas are used to compute the effective income tax bracket depending on the form of ownership.

EXHIBIT 3-11

Investors and Lenders

Investor	Requirements	Lender	Requirements
Venture capital company	Firm has potential for high growth in revenue and profits Provide capital and expertise Has investment limits	Commercial institution (bank, savings and loan, personal loan co.)	Personal, economic, and management Criteria Limit on amount of capital Generally need collateral Business plan helpful
		Government agency	Strict criteria to qualify for loan Lends money only for specific purpose(s) (i.e., different agencies for different types of loans)
Large business company	Provide capital and expertise Search for firm with stable ROI		Time delays to receive loan
Friend/ relative	No general requirements Percent of return generally agreed to Should have written, not a rized agreement	Friend/relative/ professional person	Flexible terms Recommend written not a rized agreement
Foundation	Specific criteria for investment Investment limits Not usually done	Small business investment company (SBIC)	Licensee of federal government Makes loans up to 20 percent of current capital at interest rate below market

			Loan is balloon payment, unsecured, with receivers having limited liability
			Targets of SBICs are socially or economically disadvantaged entrepreneurs
Professional Person	Looking for tax shelter Wish high growth on money No general criteria for investment Should have notarized written agreement	Small Business Administration	Loans to independent owner whose annual receipts do not exceed $2 million to $8Million Loans are primarily for working capital
		Life insurance Policies	Borrow most of policy's cash; surrender value below market interest rates
Investment banker	Matches private investor's contributions Specific guide lines for investment	Credit union	Loan below market interest Rate Can borrow on life insurance issued through union
Investor Founder	Requirements Lender Puts up funds to begin operations Invests money to accrue larger return through his or her efforts Contribution used to secure more capital		

The combination of lenders and investors who can fulfill your financial needs is unique to your situation. The decision about seeking such capital is not. As with many other elements of operating a business, there is a tradeoff between the low-risk, high-disclosure attributes of an investment and the high-risk, low-disclosure attributes of a loan. Equity investors are owners of the consulting firm and are thereby entitled to a voice in the conduct of business affairs, whereas debt financiers can restrict consulting firms from pursuing other financing or expansion opportunities. In fact, even if these lenders do not limit the capital formation, the presence of substantial obligations will often discourage other creditors or lenders from providing the additional financing that a consulting firm may sorely need.

Therefore, one way to manage this trade-off is to consider equity or debt capital as a resource of East resort. Before pursuing any outside sources of funds, efforts should be made to keep your internal operations financially sound. Such efforts include:

- Instituting cost controls to keep better track of costs and to eliminate waste (see Chapter Eight),
- Liquidating assets or selling more stock as needed
- Extending line(s) of credit
- Refining current investments and/or loans

Each of these measures is used to sustain the solvency of the consulting business. If additional funds are needed, you can pursue the investor route, the lender route, or both.

Sample Task V

You have been in business for 16 months. Your clients are chronically late with payments. To meet your expenses, you need $10,000 over the next six months. How would you meet this need? What options would you pursue? Why? In what order would you pursue them? What are your contingencies in case the options do not yield capital? How personal might your borrowing get?

SUMMARY AND CONCLUSION

In essence, you have just completed a short course in the fundamentals of beginning a small business. The decisions about firm structure, planning, and financing are keys to establishing any business. Your consultancy design will affect your marketing approach, your interaction with potential clients, and

---

EXHIBIT 3-12

Determination Criteria for Securing a Loan

Personal
A profile of the prospective borrower is drawn based on the consultant owner's prior experience, capability, and character. The profile is informal, but reflects the consultant's professional manner.

Management
The business acumen of the prospective borrower is assessed to see how well he or she has been managing the firm. The experience and assistance of the other owners (if any) are included in the analysis.

Loan
The amount of funds needed is stated together with the precise uses of the money. The owner also describes the repayment timetable.

Business Plan
The firm's business plan, showing the amount of capital committed to the business, the cash flow aver the last quarter (if available), the projected cash flow over the next quarter, and further cost justification for the stated capital requirement, is submitted.

Economic Conditions
The general state of the economy, other loans pending, and prior experiences with consulting firms are taken into account in deciding whether to grant the loan.

---

the way proposals are written, contracts are secured, services are provided, fees are set, and later, the manner in which the consultancy grows. Keep in mind that your business not only reflects your current position in the marketplace but also the medium through which future financial, professional, and service growth can occur. For this reason you should consult with an attorney and an accountant to choose the appropriate legal form and to determine the best ways and means to manage the consultancy. The next chapter expands on the "means" with a discussion of marketing.

Chapter Four

Marketing

Attracting the Potential Client

SNAPSHOT

At this point you have stated your reasons for being a consultant and defined your business structure. With the groundwork laid, you must now turn to the heart of the consulting business-getting clients.

The first section of this chapter shows you how to define the services you are selling and the clientele who are purchasing them. Understanding the likely match and mismatch of services to clients helps determine a successful marketing method. In this chapter a sample marketing method is presented.

The first step to getting a foot in the client's door is the brochure - a terse pamphlet that neatly and pointedly describes the who, what, why, how, and when of your consulting practice. At a glance, the client can glean a basic sense of your skills, experience, and background. This initial contact is then furthered by letters, telephone conversations, or visits. Your object remains the same—setting up a full-scale meeting to discuss the feasibility of your providing services. At such a meeting, your appearance and presentation will give the client a clear sense of whether your services are necessary, and if so, whether you should provide them. At the same time, you have a decision to make. As discussed in the special topic, there are times when the consultant may decide that a particular client situation is too risky to pursue. How well you lay the foundation bears directly on your outcome.

So let's begin.

DEVELOPING A MARKETING STRATEGY

Given your decision to sell consulting services, the next question is, how? To answer this, let's first discuss the services you want to provide. Exhibit 4-1 describes some of the variables that make up a consultation. Exhibit 4-2 shows how these variables can be translated into .a concrete consulting practice.

Sample Task I

Study Exhibit 4-1 and form a picture for each kind of consulting you wish to do. Then ask yourself the following questions:

- Are the services portrayed concisely?
- Can the client easily understand what is being offered?
- Do these services accurately reflect my skills, interests, and experience?
- How well do my services match the potential client's needs, and are they competitive with other consultants?

The procedure you have just gone through is a never-ending one in consulting. To have top-quality and readily usable services, you need to modify, redefine, and augment them constantly.

Second, knowing who your likely clients are is equally important to understanding the services they may need. Exhibit 4-3 describes the factors to consider when deciding which clients to target. Exhibit 4-4 gives examples of sample clients.

Sample Task II

Study Exhibit 4-3 and write down a short yet detailed description of your potential clients. Now ask yourself:
- Are these the kinds of clients 1 want to serve? Why?
- Are my clients likely to have little in common or much in common?
- How timely are the services being offered to these clients?

This exercise will give you a clearer idea of when and how your services can be used. The simplest service to sell is the one that the client wants to buy.

Sample Task III

On a single page, list the services you wish to sell, to whom you want to self them, and what your qualifications are for doing so. Show this page to a

EXHIBIT 4-1

Service Characterization

Types	Frequency	Variety	Quality	Timeliness	Provision	Output	Payment
General management	At one time	One	Unique	In response to crisis	Given alone	Report	Retainer
Finance	In segments	Multiple	Well known	To foster longterm change	Given with other consultants	Computer run	Contract
Personnel/ employment					Other	Workshop	Other
Techical/ technology analyses							
Marketing							
Data processing							
Construction/ maintenance							
Policy studies							
Organization evaluation							
Production or program assessment							
Training							
Advisory							
Editorial etc.							

EXHIBIT 4-2

Service Examples

1. organization Development Consultant assesses organization to ascertain strengths and weaknesses of all primary functions and ways to cope w2 change Off-the-shelf techniques are used in producing a white' paper Consultant is under contract.
2. Executive Recruitment Consultant seeks chief executive officers (CEOs) or nonprofit organization. Has unique cross-exchange program of introducing candidates to clients, and vice versa. Working alone consultant receives a finder's fee, a percentage of a CEO's first 'year salary
3. Quality Control Consultants in a loose consortium provide independent firm* w T production of new equipment for a communication firm. Working on a retainer, each consultant gives both his or her diagnosis and that of at least one other
4. Employee Training. Consultant provides intensive seminars in editing and report writing. Training is done over multi week periods using interactive instruction. Consultant's contract is used. Services provided alone or in combination with a graphic artist and a production editor.

---

colleague and ask the person to comment, to be a "devil's advocate." Make notes.

Now, in two sentences, define your marketing method.

Once you have defined your services and your potential clients, you are ready to market, market, market. Yet there is one important factor that, if left unsaid, would keep services from reaching clients. That factor is you.

Exhibit 4-5 lists some primary questions you need to ask yourself to build a successful marketing method. The answers to Exhibit 4-5, plus the previous characterizations of Exhibits 4-1 through 44, give you the tools needed for constructing a marketing method.

Next, Exhibit 4-6 addresses how a need for a service is fulfilled, outlining the desire tos atisfy the client need and the consultant's limitations in doing so. As we discussed in Chapter Three, the amount of time spent obtaining the first income is in direct proportion to the initial investment of consultant time and resources. Second, your marketing method's success is based on how many qualified leads you can make in the time allotted and the capture ratio (percent of contracts won to new clients).

EXHIBIT 4-3

Client Characterization

Sector	Organization	Administration	Skills	Needs	Client Size	Audience
Public	Large	Complex	Technical	General	Individual	Minority
Private	Medium	Structured	Managerial	Specific	Group	General
Institu-tional	Small	Simple	Combination	Mixed	Intergroup	
					Other	

Previous Contracts with Consultants	Location	Cultural/Language Differences	Initial Contact
None	Local	None	Personal
1–3	National	None	Referral
Over 3	International	Many	New

EXHIBIT 4-4

Client Examples[1]

1. Organization Development. Client is office of consumer assistance for a federal agency. Consultant is called in by director to prepare a report demonstrating more effective management practices. The agency director and his assistants review the report and are in charge of implementing its findings. The client had never used a consultant before, but decided to at the suggestion of a colleague in an equivalent position elsewhere in the agency.
2. Executive Recruitment Clients are small health maintenance organizations. The consultant works with the board of governors to find the right chief executive officer (CEO). One client never used this service before, since its former CEO was the founder of the firm.
3. Quality Control. Clients are project managers in new product development of large, multinational corporations. The needs are multiple—a fast, credible design for quality control, which must then be presented to technical management and staff in Japan, Brazil, and Egypt, where production facilities are located. Most project managers have used outside consulting before.
4. Employee Training. Clients are lower- to middle-level managers of computer consultant firms. Consultant provides technical and managerial services. Most firms have used consulting assistance before.

---

[1]In parallel to the examples of Exhibit 4-2.

EXHIBIT 4-5

Consultant Characterization

Skills
- What abilities do you have for consulting in general?
- What are your capabilities for doing the specific consulting noted?

Experience
- What has been your exposure to consulting?
- Describe briefly the types of consulting activities you have been involved in (including both successes and failures).

Motivation
- Why do you want to go into consulting?
- What do you hope to gain? What could you lose?

Comparison
- How are you and your potential clients alike? Not alike?
- How are you and your "rival" consultants alike?
- What can you do to gain a competitive edge?

Devotion
- How much time are you willing to put in initially to market clients?
- How many clients are you willing to see?
- How long will you give yourself to secure a contract?

Outcome: Briefly summarize your attitude toward marketing.

EXHIBIT 4-6

Sample Marketing Method

1. Perceived Need. Assistance in the formation of professional associations.
2. Rationale. New groups are forming associations, and existing organizations are reorganizing. But few, if any, executives possess experience in forming and operating associations. Also, the costs of managing an association are rising.
3. Target Clientele. Associations that are less than one year old, or associations about to form.
4. Information Sources
   - Business sections of daily newspapers in "association" cities (Washington, D.C., Chicago, and New York; and secondarily, Atlanta, Houston, Los Angeles, Boston, and Denver) o Association executives
   - Association Executives
   - Personal contacts in professional groups and societies
   - American Society of Association Executives
5. Services Provided
   - Form decision techniques
   - Evaluate location

- Share management services
- Plan and design office
- Design recruitment and marketing techniques and campaigns
- Set up liaisons with other associations
- Comply with regulations
- Devise organization and finance structures and control mechanisms
- Coordinate publicity and convention programs

6. Time Investment
   - Continuous effort until initial contract secured
   - Three-quarter-time effort until second contract secured
   - Objective: One day per week in direct marketing, one day per week promoting, and three days of contract work

7. Benchmarks
   - First contract within 60 days of marketing
   - Second contract within 90 days of marketing
   - A first contract won from four to seven leads
   - Additional contract won from three to five contacts

What do you use to carry out a marketing method? The answer is the brochure. This tool is the bridge between goal setting and goal realization.

It is your calling card, the way to get to see clients. The brochure also gives you credibility and effectively establishes rapport with a client. In addition, the design and use of a brochure gives you experience handling advertising and promotion (discussed further in Chapter Seven).

How do you design a brochure? There are no set steps. But there are some design and editorial guidelines that you should follow:

1. Focus on a central message. For example, I understand your concern, I can alleviate your difficulties to your satisfaction, and my services are competent, competitive, and guaranteed.
2. Keep the text short and simple. Use definite, specific and jargon free language. Use the active voice, keeping your sentences brief.
3. List your credentials. In terse language, state only your abilities and results relevant to the client audience.
4. Describe your previous experience. Again, relate this information to your audience. Lack of experience does not hinder marketing. State the range of assistance offered.
5. Convey your operating philosophy. Describe your methods of practice, fee determination, ethics, and other relevant factors.
6. Use strong graphics. Your type should be easy to read. Front and back covers should be eye-catching. Study other brochures to help you

decide on using a logo, graphic displays, horizontal or vertical format, and so on.

7. Test the brochure. Circulate the draft to colleagues and friends. Ask the readers if they understand what the service is, why it is being offered, who can use it, and under what conditions. Now, ask yourself: How well does the brochure reflect the image I wish to portray?

8. Edit, rewrite, prepare final copy, and print. Your first brochure is your first attempt-with more to come as the business evolves.

Exhibit 4–7 is an example of a brochure used for an initial, business capturing endeavor. The language is concise and pointed. The copy includes a lead-in, a message, and details on how to contact the consultant.

EXHIBIT 4-7

Beginning Brochure

(Front Cover)

New Associations—
Can We Take the Risk?
In the last ten years, the number of associations has doubled the support services for management has declined. Associations are the life-blood of professional development, the heartbeat of congressional lobbying, and the watchdog of successful and profitable operations for member organizations

To enable these functions to occur amid a changing economic, regulatory, and professional environment, effective and responsive management is needed. Our services are specifically oriented to those groups of professionals who wish to form new associations without initial management kinks and inefficiencies.

(Back Cover)

For further information about this singular opportunity, please contact:

Susan Duit
(312) 822-2777: day
(312) 862-1257: night

or write
Assoc. Form, Inc.
1616 Professional Blvd
Evanston, IL 60200

We offer custom-tailored services to design and implement startup systems for smooth and effective association management

(Inside, First Page)

Service Program
Our goals are to foster the following institutional abilities:

- To start up a new association in a timely and cost-effective manner.
- To build contacts in expanding membership
- To create liaisons with other professional associations
- To install public relations, publicity, accounting, education, and convention programs
- To plan for the long-term health of the association

(Inside, Second Page)

Service Package
The achievement of these goals requires nothing short of a comprehensive, yet economical effort to launch new organizations. Such a plan would include:

- Organization feasibility study
- Custom formation plan for the New association
- Startup and organization scheme
- Cost-effective management options
- Office planning
- Membership campaign strategies
- Bridge building with other associations
- Staffing and financial control techniques
- First-quarter review and critique
- Subsequent monitoring and evaluation

Exhibit 4-8, an advanced brochure, contains these features plus brief statements about the consultant's experience, former clients, and operating philosophy.

When you are not there to represent yourself, your brochure will do the job. It will be read and distributed. And as shown below and in Chapter Seven, the brochure is the cornerstone of an effective marketing, advertising, and promotional campaign, Create it wisely.

Sample Task IV

Develop a brochure for a consulting service that you have little intention of pursuing. Set it aside for a few days and then come back and critique it.

EXHIBIT 4-8

Advanced Brochure

(Front Cover)

AFI
Associations Management:
Help or Hindrance?

Today there are more association then ever before. Similarly, there is a greater need for effective management and liaison. Operating Costs are going up, competing activities are on the rise, and the complexity of doing business increases each day.

In this milieu comes a fresh look. Assoc. Form is here to alleviate management deficiencies stimulate association liaison, and enhance organizational activities and involvement For beginning or existing associations, our services could be the leg up needed for survival.

We offer custom services, carefully tailored and accurately implemented significantly improve the internal and external management of associations.

(Back Cover)

To discover how you can make these significant improvements, please contact:

Susan Duit
c/o Assoc. Form, Inc
1616 Professional Blvd.
Evanston, IL 60200

Or call toll-free:
(800)999-3344

(Inside, First Page)

Service Capability
As an outside resource, we bring state-of-the-art techniques and experience to the association executive. Our program includes, but is not limited to:

* Concept study
* Organization plan
* Communications package
* On-site startup

(Inside, Second Page)

Prior Experience
Management advice and assistance has recently been given to:

* National Association of Retired Persons
* State Council of Governments
* Institute for American Universities
* National Child Day Care Association

- Unique publicity and membership campaign
- Cost control techniques » Self-review marketing and critique

  Your needs are treated individually and completely. Prior experience with more than a dozen contacts shows that timely interaction produces results that work.

- Society for Neuroscience

  Operating Philosophy

  We practice in the highest ethical manner, not working for two competing clients, or transferring information without client consent. As a certified member of the Consulting Professional Association, we uphold its practice standards. References are available on request. Our major concern is the timely transfer of programs. Thus we work on a time-and-materials basis (either your contract or ours).

  The consulting services we give are guaranteed to provide insight and effective change. Our challenge is working with you to implement these improvements

What insights have you learned that can assist you in preparing a professional brochure?

GAINING CLIENT ENTRY

You have now identified the services you wish to offer, the general client community to receive them, and your strategy for marketing them; also, you have prepared your primary marketing tool-the brochure. It appears that you are ready to "walk into a client's office and make a sale. "Right? Of course, right!

But hold on. Whom do you contact? How do you reach them? How do you set up an appointment? What will you say? Why will the prospective client listen to you? How will you make the sale? To gain the client's attention, you need to remember that most clients distrust consultants; mistrust their services; don't know how to use consulting services effectively; won't let outsiders examine their activities; or fail to realize that they have a problem. Therefore, any answers you get must be directed at overcoming the client's resistance to your presence.

There are three ways to contact clients-a cold-call, a referral, or a personal contact. All three work. All produce results. Prior associates, colleagues, or clients serve as the most likely pool from which new business can arise. Referrals by colleagues or personal friends are an excellent means of entry provided that your contact introduces you effectively. The cold call is the most difficult way to contact a client. After garnering names from listing services, directories, associations, conference attendance sheets, and so forth, specific client names are extracted depending on the prospect's business and geographic location. The method(s) you try initially will depend on your experience, old contacts, and ability to make new contacts. The less difficult it is to meet and talk with someone, the sooner direct marketing can occur. (Additional ways to make client contact are described in Chapter Seven.)

The January 1979 issue of the Howard L. Shenson Report, a business periodical for the independent consultant, describes a fascinating ploy to attract old colleagues to your new business. Shenson suggests that the new consultant select close professional associates from different firms and tell them about his or her move to consulting. Next, ask to have lunch with each associate to find out his or her opinion of the opportunities and limitations in the respective vocational areas. After listening to your "experts," you will be better equipped to offer services that fulfill their needs.

Alternatively, for previous acquaintances who are prospects, an informal gathering could be arranged to present your services. This demonstration can occur through a professional association, at a convention, or as a special marketing activity. In both cases, the prospective clients are trustworthy and in potential need of your services. Let's now see how you make one-on-one marketing happen.

Personal associate. Using either the "warm-up" technique described above, a phone call, or a visit, make an appointment to discuss the client's concerns and your services. Be polite, straightforward, sincere, and open.

An example of an appointment call is given in Exhibit 4-9. This conversation illustrates the informal, direct, and considerate demeanor that establishes a positive rapport with the would-be client. Let your prospect decide on the date of the meeting and the time. Finally, no two appointment conversations have exactly the same content.

Referral. Here the consultant uses a third party, a person who usually knows both parties, to expedite a meeting. The two of you should decide what communication mode-letter, telephone, or visit-will enhance your chances to meet with the prospect.

For example, assume that your mutual contact says that she has spoken to the would-be client and that he will be in his office Thursday afternoon.

Come Thursday, you decide to pay him an initial visit. Exhibit 4-10 shows you what could transpire. Here the tone is formal. With either response, you should state your intention to follow up with a phone call. The third party's

---

EXHIBIT 4-9

Phone Call to Arrange for Appointment with Prospect

Consultant:	Larry? This is Steve. Do you have a moment, or have I caught you at a bad time?
Prospect	Yes, what's on your mind?
Consultant:	I have recently started my own consulting practice, as I mentioned to you not long ago. My practice is primarily education and training. The type of programs I'm involved with include training consultants to further their consulting activities. My programs are not "canned"; each training event is oriented toward a specific situation and requirements. My purpose in speaking with you is to arrange a meeting to explore your needs. Also, at that time, we could discuss how my services could best serve your organization. This exchange should not take more than a few minutes. How does this sound to you?
Prospect:	It sounds okay, Steve, but I'd like to have some senior people sit in with me
Consultant	Certainly, Let's try to see each other next Thursday at 4:00 p.m. or next Friday at 9:00 a.m. Which would be better for you?
Prospect:	Hmm, I'm busy at both those times, but free for lunch Friday. What do you say?
Consultant	That's fine. Look forward to seeing you, Larry, and thank you:

EXHIBIT 4-10

Introductory Call on the Client

Consultant	My name is Peter Reliance, and I would like to speak with Mr. Jones (prospective client)
Secretary	Please state your purpose
Consultant	I am here to pay a visit to Mr. Jones
Secretary	Just a moment, I will ring Mr. Jones. You may go in now
Consultant	I am Peter Reliance, an independent consultant. I know you are extremely busy, but I wanted to stop by and meet you. Recently, I met a mutual colleague

	of ours, Ms. Gobet, at a seminar on government use of consultants. She spoke to me about your activities, and I appreciate her assistance in arranging this introduction. Briefly, I work in consulting training and development, primarily with government clients. I'd like to give you a call in the next few days to arrange a mutually agreeable time for further discussions. In this way I can explain to you what I do and why
Mr. Jones	Ms. Gobet is a close friend, and, yes, I would like to take the time to learn more about your services. Could you please call me at the end of next week to arrange a mutually agreeable appointment time?
Consultant: or	Fine. I'll be happy to speak with you then
Secretary:	Mr. Jones is busy and can't see you now. Could you leave your name and a number where he can contact you?
Consultant	Thank you. Here is my card. I will be in touch with Mr. Jones in a few days to arrange for an appointment.

assistance has enabled you to explain your services briefly, setting the stage for subsequent discussions,

Cold-call. This means of introduction is the riskiest, but also unavoidable — so enjoy it! No matter how you obtained the contact's name, call first to verify that he or she is still performing the same duties. Also, tell the person who you are, what you do, and why he or she is a plausible candidate for your services. In this first conversation tell the person how you found his or her name. For instance, "I am calling based on a paper you presented at such-and-such conference." Or "I saw your name in a newsletter of such-and-such organization. We are both charter members."

Or "Your name came across my desk as one of a select group of training directors. My interest and services are also in this realm." Then offer to send the prospective client your brochure, a covering letter, and any other relevant information. Keep the phone conversation short and direct (see Exhibit 4-11) and try to arrange a follow-up discussion and possible meeting, This is conveyed again in the covering letter of Exhibit 4-12.[2] The letter can also be used

---

[2]Further discussion on marketing of federal clients is given in Chapter Ten.

EXHIBIT 4-11

Phone Conversation for a Cold-Call

Consultant:	Good morning, may I please speak to Mr. Progdev?
Secretary:	Mr. Progdev is on the other line. Do you wish to hold?
Consultant	Yes, please tell him my name is Jack Cando. I am an independent consultant here in Washington, D.C:
Prospect:	Hello, this is Jules Progdev
Consultant	Good morning, this is Jack Cando. I am calling you this morning based on an initial discussion with Helen Train well in your management development branch. I am an independent consultant specializing in the training area
Prospect	How can we help, Mr. Cando?
Consultant:	For the last two years, I have been involved in training government clients in how to use consulting resources more effectively. The workshops I put together give the participants a unique opportunity to strengthen their communication and administration skills in dealing with consultants. In your agency there is enough contracting to warrant consideration of this' training activity. I have prepared a packet of materials that details the services offered, and, if you like, I would be pleased to send you a copy.
Prospect	I am intrigued by what you have said and would like to take a close look at your information. Do send me two packets as my colleague, Joan Skill up in administration, would also be interested in your training.
Consultant	Fine. I'll put the training information in the mail by this evening. Then, I'll phone back in two weeks to ensure that the mails work and to see what the next step should be
Prospect:	That's fine. Thank you for your time, and I look forward to receiving your materials

---

as an initial communication device. Your first sentence might read: "Have you considered that the current market for federal consulting services may actually be in an underutilized state?"

Enclose your business card or a brochure with your full name, address, and phone number. After sending a letter, call the client prospect until you both agree on a suitable time for an initial meeting, or determine that your services are not required. You will probably have to make several calls.

EXHIBIT 4-12

Follow-up Letter to Initial Client Phone Call

Consultant Letterhead

Date

Mr. Jules Progdev, Head
Productivity Improvement Branch
888 Constitution Avenue, N.W.
Federal Agency PQR
Washington, DC 20076

Dear Mr. Progdev:

It was a pleasure to speak with you about consulting training. As your colleague, Jan Burcrat, recently remarked at a seminar on "Government's Need for Support Contractors," the federal market may expand rapidly in the future, although procurement controls could tighten. To meet the needs of a stricter, competitive market, higher quality is required. Quality means both people and their services. Raising productivity can be done through multiple means; one of these is training.

From the accompanying brochure and needs analysis, a workshop can be constructed on how federal program officials can better utilize the services of consultants. This tailor-made course can either augment an existing training component or form a new learning segment. Further, the learning segments can be either one- or two-day seminars, three- or four-week short courses, or a combination, depending on the preference of your office or the various departmental areas you serve. Participation is a key communication technique through exercises, question-and-answer periods, and diagnostic sessions about current problems and concerns.

This is not to say that such training can be all things to all people. It cannot. Instead, the learning experience can provide better bridges between program officials and contracting officers, as well as program officials and consultants, so that program mandates can be executed more effectively. To demonstrate this principle, an example of a training workshop is enclosed.

I look forward to your response to this letter and training material once immediate administrative concerns are resolved,

Sincerely,
Jack Cando
Independent Consultant

JC/mm
Enclosure

Perseverance and flexibility are important, but so are patience and politeness in reminding the prospect of your interest in offering consulting services.

Sample Task V

Closely monitor your next prospect to see how you make initial contact and the tools you use to arrange a meeting. Could you have changed the order of methods used? Take notes during your phone calls; how could they be improved? What is your initial impression of the prospect? What are your reservations and motivations for making a sale?

The methods we have discussed are predicated on the consultant taking and sustaining the initiative toward arranging a client meeting. As your reputation grows, the demand for your services will increase and potential clients will request your services. It is a proud moment when this happens, but do not expect it. If it occurs, tell the client about your services, your background, and how you think the services will, in general, enhance the client's organization. More specific information will be given during the client/consultant assessment of your services (described further in the following pages).

The exhibits depicted here describe positive outcomes. Two additional comments are in order. If the client says, "Thank you, but no thank you," then you politely say that you hope your services can be of use in the future.

Second, if after sufficient communication, the would-be client is either undecided or wishes to postpone any further discussion, the consultant can cease marketing until a more conducive time. In closing the conversation with the client, attempt to discover when that time is.

In addition, no matter what the outcome of the entry phase, keep records. Marketing information can be kept in a three by five-inch file box.

For each prospect, fill out a separate card, as in Exhibit 4-13. Keep a record of the dates at which various actions occur. It is a good idea periodically to collate all leads, prospects, and contracts in a review sheet. Such a sheet (shown in Exhibit 4-14) can be used to determine the benchmarks of your marketing method, as well as the accounting, which will be addressed in depth in Chapter Eight.

Case Example 4-1: The Story Teller

John, a colleague of mine, has a distinctive entry style with a prospective client. He usually acquires one or two facts about the client's situation, and then says to the client something like:

EXHIBIT 4-13

Sample Card for a Prospect

Name _____   Manner contact made _____

Phone number _____

Name of client organization _____   Address _____

To be contacted . . . _____

Letter sent _____   Phone call _____

Visit _____

Other _____ Appointment _____

Appointment outcome _____

Potential contract amount _____

Current status._____

_____ _____   Comments and impressions . . . _____

EXHIBIT 4-14

Marketing at a Glance

Date _____
Completion

Leads	Date	Prospects	Status/Date	Con-tracts	Amount Date	
Total Leads		Total Prospects	Potential Contract Value		Total Contracts	Project Value
Benchmark			Actual Achievement		Differences	Comments
1.						
2.						
3.						
4.						

"Your situation reminds me precisely of another consulting assignment I once did. It just so happens that the client also was experiencing these troubles and needed my expertise to get out of a jam. Here's what happened. . . ." john then finishes weaving his yarn of enticement to the client. No, the consultant is not broke; on the contrary, he has a thriving business.

I asked if he ever came across poorly to certain kinds of people: The answer given was: "Well-uh, yes, women especially and young managers seem to be unimpressed. If anything, they think I'm wasting their time." "Then what do you do?" I asked. His reply was expected: "I usually save an exploit for the end, just to leave a provocative impression with them." The upshot, though, is that this person told more stories than sold contracts-many more.

MEETING WITH THE CLIENT FOR THE FIRST TIME

The purpose of the first meeting is to define the prospect's interest, to discuss the consultant's procedure and resources in dealing with this interest, and to establish a working relationship. These objectives are realized concurrently. Thus you need to be prepared to address and respond to the entire situation. Three elements influence your performance: (1) appearance, (2) presentation, and (3) interaction.

Appearance. In your first encounter with a prospect, you gain an initial impression and make one. A primary element is appearance. Some consultants use appearance as their calling card by wearing loud colors, dark glasses, or coming in "wind blown." The rationale is easy-the flashy consultant figures that the would-be client will remember his or her unique dress style. It is true. But will potential clients remember this consultant in a positive light? Probably not. To create a relaxed atmosphere at the first meeting, you should wear conventional, well-fitting clothes, be neat, and be yourself, emphasizing the positive aspects of your image. The importance of appearance is indirectly proportional to the number of interactions with a client. The longer the consultant knows the client, works with the client, and feels comfortable with him or her, the less influence appearance plays in the outcome of the meeting.

Presentation. Although no two first sessions are the same, there is a four-part procedure to "sell the client," which has proven to be successful. It consists of something like this:

Warm-up. The consultant comes into the client's office, first expressing appreciation at having the opportunity, while noting the time constraint both parties are under. Then the consultant briefly reviews his or her background, including education, experience, areas of concentration, and former clients. A few comments on the prospective client's firm or agency are also included to show consultant interest and insight. Then the consultant asks for questions from the client and asks the client questions, if appropriate.

Overview. Having established a "climate," the consultant now presents the essence of his or her services. There are as many ways to do this as there are marketing guides. However, one means that has proven effective is the preparation of a Needs Analysis. After explaining the basic services, the consultant suggests preparing a Needs Analysis to discover whether these services fit the client's situation. Exhibit 4-15, an example of such a Needs Analysis, is used to gather basic data about the client and the organization. The consultant explains the content of the Needs Analysis form and what results are expected from its completion-that is, a better understanding of the real issues requiring assistance.

Issue clarification. The Needs Analysis form is filled out jointly by consultant and client. Using Exhibit 4-15, the object is to uncover the client's concerns and how, if at all, the consultant can be of assistance. A Needs Analysis should be completed whether the client has sought out the consultant or vice versa. But do not gather the information for this form at the expense of your relationship with the client. To sustain your rapport, restate

---

EXHIBIT 4-15

Needs Analysis Form

Client name _____   Date. _____

Firm or agency name _____   Phone number _____

Number of employees _____   Firm address _____

Focus issue _____   _____

Brief description _____   Basic purpose or product _____

Prior efforts to handle problem _____

Client's current objectives _____

Previous use of consultants _____

Current perspective on consultants _____

Consultant's initial evaluation _____

Consulting services of use here _____

Advantages of services _____

Disadvantages of services

client perspectives, interject supportive comments, and be nonjudgmental throughout. The object is to reach an understanding of whether you can work with the prospective client. To do so, communicate simply, directly, and succinctly. Simple, clear English is a powerful tool. You need not complicate things with obtuse, jargon-laden language. Also, listen to what the client is saying, distinguish between what the real issue is as opposed to what the client perceives it to be. Give the client ample time to talk without cutting the person off. Repeat major points that were discussed. The feedback assures the client that you have heard what he or she has been saying.

Closure. At the close of the meeting, leave a copy of the Needs Analysis with the potential client. The prospect can study it, consider the relative costs and benefits of the proposed consultant services, relate such services to other concerns, and then let you know his or her decision. The bottom line is whether the prospect thinks that your services are required now and what form they will take. Further, there are ways to improve communication and keep the conversation going. For example:

- If the client is accepting, attempt to move the conversation toward discussing a contractual relationship.
- If the client is skeptical, take a different track and show that this skepticism is a permissible and expected stance.
- If the client is hostile, liven up the dialogue with a joke, and move on to demonstrating the advantages of your services.
- If the hostility persists or the client is bored, point this out and suggest an alternative day and time for continued discussions.

Sample Task VI

Plan a marketing meeting. Set down the topics to be covered, the tools employed, the communication skills available, and the characteristics/impressions of the would-be client. Find a colleague or friend. Have this person play the client, and you be the consultant. Role-play the first meeting. Then critique each other's performance. What have you learned about becoming more sensitive to the communication aspect of marketing?

After your initial meeting, write a succinct letter of thanks, reiterating your desire to offer assistance. Later, call the client to learn his or her decision on your offer. If need be, set up another short meeting to refine your efforts. Make any supportive comments, such as citing examples inside or outside the client's organization where such services are being used, past successes or service use, pertinent shortcomings, and how these services will fit into the organization's operations, objectives, or management development.

In the next chapter, competitive contracting is discussed. The principles articulated there are an extension of what has been said herein.

Win, lose, or draw, you should conduct a debriefing to determine the strengths and weaknesses of your marketing effort. This can be accomplished by merely jotting down notes, filling out a form, or completing a formal, written assessment. The purpose is to find out your problem are as for example, information gaps, rapport, state of client organizations, mismatch of services with organizational needs, and so on. Also note the positive points of the encounter, This information serves as valuable knowledge for future, more successful marketing efforts.

SPECIAL TOPIC: TURNING DOWN A CONSULTING OPPORTUNITY

For a beginner, the thought of saying "no" to a client seems contradictory.

However, on closer inspection, we find a healthy rationale for refusing consulting work. Every assignment you do contributes to your reputation.

Thus, any consulting activity-particularly an initial engagement-that could harm you should be avoided. There are no hard-and-fast indicators, but there are some signals to look for:

Personality clash. Consultant and client chemistry may not be conducive to forming a working relationship. Try to improve the interaction by talking about it. If this does not work, suggest an alternative consultant.

Scope of work. If the effort outlined by the client is too large, complex, costly, and/or unrealistically scheduled, consultant and client can attempt to renegotiate the assignment terms without fundamentally changing the objectives or benefits of the consultation. If this is only partially effective, the consultant can specify other support persons to assist with the effort. If, together, these measures do not allow the consultant to do a high-quality job, an alternative consultant could be mentioned to the client.

Working style. The assignment may call for the consultant to behave and to perform in ways that would compromise his or her independence, objectivity, and integrity. *Corrective measures* (as above) could include redefining the scope of the work and the consultant/client relationship. If both are not possible, the consultant should seriously consider declining the offer.

Conflict of interest. In the same vein as above, measures are taken to eliminate such conflict. If they prove to be unsuccessful, the consultant should refuse the assignment.

Financial stability, If, for any reason, the financial status of the client organization appears shaky, the consultant should thoroughly examine the client's ability to pay before signing a contract. If such an examination was denied or any subsequent pertinent information withheld, there would be grounds for rejecting the assignment.

You will probably not encounter these situations every day. But since you want to provide high-quality services at a reasonable rate, any obstacles should be immediately resolved before committing yourself. Use discretion in handling these matters, but also seek competent advice as need be.

Case Example 4-2: To Turn Back, Turn Down?

The instance described below is not peculiar to one firm. I know of several private firms that Rave an annual budget cycle for procuring goods and services. These firms go out to bid in October and award contracts by February 1 for the entire calendar year.

Company BCE issued solicitations for various technical support, including project analyses, computer assistance, and training. I submitted a response to the training services request during the budget cycle. In January, I was asked to come in for negotiations. Having received word that I passed, I concluded that the next step was the award. How wrong I was! Five months passed before the award was made. BCE offered me 30 percent less than I negotiated far and truncated three tasks. Two days later I received additional instructions asking if I would substitute two remaining tasks for two others.

Five months late, thousands of dollars less than my initial offer, and a new scope of work. Were these grounds for rejecting the consulting assignment? I went to negotiate a final contract only to discover that the firm's procurement procedure had changed. I could only do the work one task at a time on separate accounting vouchers. The handwriting was on the wall. I sent them a polite note that kept the door open—but only to better experiences.

SUMMARY AND EXTENSION

This chapter has looked closely at marketing, a subject that often receives cursory treatment. Often, initial efforts to meet with a prospective client are assumed to occur as a matter of course driven by the desire for initial contracts. Or, the lack of knowledge or motivation about selling an intangible service assumes that someone else will make the contacts. In either case, the consultant passes the buck. Understanding how to overcome your resistance and do your own marketing can give you insight into how to work through the client's resistance to using your services. So, here a step-by-step approach is presented, starting with the development of a marketing method and ending with the client's decision whether to ask for a proposal. Exhibits shed light on such glossed-over areas as the ways a brochure changes, how a consultant gets to see a prospective client, and how to make the first meeting a successful one. The next chapter is fundamental to the consulting assignment because without a secure and reasonable contract, no services can be given. We have laid the groundwork for that stage in trying to ensure a mutually satisfying and beneficial consulting experience.

Chapter Five

Securing the Contract

SNAPSHOT

If you are going to make it in consulting, you need income an activity. This chapter presents a no-nonsense method for obtaining a contract. What you are after is how to turn your previous effort into a working relationship with a client. Therefore, this chapter will demonstrate the skills you will need, including deciding to bid on consulting work, writing and presenting a proposal, negotiating terms of the assignment, and turning these tasks into a secured contract. With these primary tools, plus additional marketing experience, the long-term health of your consulting practice can be assured.

DECIDING TO SEEK CLIENT ASSIGNMENTS

You might think that this section should be entitled "The Client Decision to Seek Consultant Assistance," but given your effort so far, this step is up to you. A client request for a proposal will run the gamut from a formal document (as with the federal government), to a letter as an extension of the Needs Analysis, to only verbal input. Generally, a prospective client will send you a letter requesting a written proposal describing your methods of operation and expected results. Exhibit 5-1 shows a sample client request. To evaluate the client's request realistically, you first need to answer the questions listed in Exhibit 5-2. If you answer "no" to any of them, you need further information from either the client or some other source. For instance, consider the question about an adequate return from the payment scheme. If you feel that the payment scheme leaves you with minimal profit or no profit at the end of the engagement, suggest a more appropriate payment scheme to the client. You must inform the client of the conditions under which you will bid.

Exhibit 5-3 illustrates a consultant evaluation of the sample request described in Exhibit 5-2. The important point in an evaluation is to jot down all of your impressions before you expend any effort submitting a proposal. If you decide not to respond to the request, write a polite letter declining the invitation, stating your reasons for refusing the bid, suggestions of how the client can enhance the request, and a sentence or two stating your intention to meet with the client in the future. Such a letter keeps the door open for future work.

EXHIBIT 5-1

Client Request for Consulting Assistance

Objectives
- To devise an evaluation method for employee turnover, e
- To assess the variations in employee turnover in different departments using this method.
- To develop an early-warning procedure for sensing employee dissatisfaction.

Rationale
Our company has been plagued with chronic high turnover. It is our desire to demonstrate an immediate reduction in the termination rate by all prudent means possible. Much discussion has already ensued but with few positive results.

Time Period
- To commence work one week after signature of contract,
- To terminate work six months later.

Level of Effort
One and one-half person-years.

Estimated Resources
- Two people,
- Computer time.
- Office/clerical/typing/reproduction expenses.

Proposed Contract

Fixed-price effort not to exceed $72,000.

EXHIBIT 5-2

To Bid or Not to Bid

Relevance
- What areas of competency will the assignment call for?
- How will the assignment relate to my prior experience? Will it be a repeat of a previous assignment, an extension of work performed to date, or a state-of-the-art challenge?
- In what ways will my professional reputation be enhanced by doing this assignment?

Timing
- What conflicts could inhibit my beginning the assignment on time and/ or completing all the specified tasks?
- Is the time frame realistic for successfully finishing the proposed work?
- Does the order of the specified consulting activities allow for expedient completion of the effort?
- Will I have time to maintain ongoing client relationships and marketing activity?

Completeness
- Are all the necessary items for a sound response included in the bid?
- What additional resources would be required to do the work, and how would I obtain them?
- What potential ethical and logistical concerns should I be aware of in carrying out this assignment?

Pricing
- Can the work requested be done for a competitive amount?
- What special arrangements need be secured to receive payment?
- Can the proposed payment scheme give me adequate return for my efforts?

Competition
- Are other consultants bidding for this assignment?
- Are there other consultants with more influence or competency than myself bidding?
- Will responding to this proposal have current or future benefits even if I am not selected?

EXHIBIT 5-3

Consultant Evaluation of Client Request:

To Improve Employee Morale

Relevance

Given my past experience with personnel concerns and my ability to relate to various levels of management, this assignment would further my skills in employee turnover analysis. My contributions to this organization would be threefold:

- Improved communication in dealing with this concern
- Reduction in the number of voluntary employee terminations
- Effective implementation of procedures for maintaining a low turnover of employees

Timing

At present, I have two other proposals and one contract that might overlap with this potential assignment. If overlap does occur and my bid is accepted, I will defer the starting date until my schedule allows primary concentration on this assignment. Further, six months is adequate time to carry through this effort.

Completeness

The basic elements are present to bid. More communication is needed with the client organization contact to ascertain whether the contract is competitive, what the time period is before award, and to let them know informally of my interest. The procedures developed for this effort will subsequently be used only with the written consent of the client. All other ethical operating principles will be upheld.

Pricing

This assignment can be done for the fixed-price amount. If my schedule dictates the employ of any subcontract assistance (with the written consent of the client), the amount may not be sufficient. Thus payment would need to come regularly throughout the effort to cover immediate expenses.

Competition

1have worked for this client before. We have a sound professional' rapport. Yet employee turnover would be a new area of direct consulting, and it has been two Years since. I worked for this client

Sample Task I

Evaluate a request for a proposal that you have received. (If you do not have one, borrow one or use Exhibit 5-7.) Discover the most important factor in bidding. Find the most important constraint to bidding. Alone, does one outweigh the other? Does a "yes" answer imply that you will decide based only on these two factors? Does a "no" answer imply that other factors are to be figured in? If you are unable to make a decision, what additional information would you need?

An evaluation of a potential assignment is incomplete by definition.

Nonetheless, your task is to discover the risks to your pocketbook and reputation and to weigh them against the monetary and professional benefits.

UNDERSTANDING A PROPOSAL

If you decide to answer the client request, your next step is to submit a response. Your response will vary depending on the client's organization, consulting services requested, and the dollar amount of the assignment. However, there are certain common components in all written proposals, as noted in Exhibit 5-4.

How do you write a solid, first-rate proposal? First, it should contain all of the elements described in Exhibit 5-4; second, it should be well organized;

EXHIBIT 5-4

Components of a Proposal

Introduction
  Current client situation
  Client understanding of issue
  Previous attempts to deal with issue

Technical Approach
  Method(s) to resolve issue
  Benefits derived and results delivered

Management Plan
  Facilities and resources
  All staff involved
  Quality control methods
  Special provisions or contingencies
  Schedule of work tasks and deliverables

Qualifications
    Education and training
    Consultant experience
Relevance of training and experience to this effort
Pricing
Procedure for calculating costs
Suggested modifications to payment type and procedure
Ancillary Items
Transmittal letter and references
Cover, title page, table of contents, and list of illustrations
Appendices

and third, it should influence the client. You can accomplish this by doing the following:

Grab the client's attention. Find a unique way to express the client's needs. Use a quote from a client document, or a graphic device-a chart or graph.

Arouse *interest.* Stress the special methods that you will use to solve the client's problems, and describe their benefits.

Turn interest into conviction. Present your services and the scope of work in realistic, logical terms. The object is not to compare your services with other consultants, but to build a strong case for yourself. This type of presentation will establish your credibility and increase your chances for success.

Ensure punctuality and completeness. Most clients prefer, if not demand, due dates and times for proposals. Make sure that yours is not late! Also, be sure to double check that every item requested by the client has been covered or noted in your proposal.

Sample Task II

Find a proposal that you have written. (If you do not have one, borrow a proposal or create an outline for one.) Critique it. Are there any flaws in content, style, organization, or pricing? Given the suggestions herein, what could you do to correct these deficiencies? Make these corrections. Now, based on the client need, is this a winning proposal? If not, can you make it into one? Why not?

EVALUATING AND SELECTING A CONSULTANT

After the deadline for proposals has passed, the client will evaluate the entries. Count on being ranked even if only one other proposal was submitted. The client evaluates each proposal according to certain requirements. Basically, the client considers three criteria: the soundness and competitiveness of the bid, the practicality of the approach, and the competence of the staff. The client selects finalists and begins negotiations with each of them.

Sample Task III

Take the proposal you examined in Sample Task II and ask a colleague to evaluate it according to factors that a client might use. Based on the evaluation, what changes would you make in the proposal? What effect would those changes have on the quality of your work, your potential profit, your reputation, and your continued interest in the project? Do you think that you should evaluate a proposal before submitting it? Why?

FORMULATING A CONSULTING CONTRACT

Before we move to the negotiation stage, it is necessary to discuss contracts. A consulting contract is a written document explaining the responsibilities and obligations of, generally, two parties in carrying out specified tasks. The two parties are the client and the consultant. The specified tasks are the consultant's services and any client support activities. How is a contract formulated? Exhibit 5-5 displays the pertinent steps, which are outlined below.

Choose the agreement form. Two main variables-pricing and ownership-determine the choice of contract. Pricing is the kind of cost structure allowed. (See Chapters Eight and Ten for a more detailed discussion.) Exhibit 5-6 outlines the major types of contract pricing and the rationale for each. As you can see, using one type over another is really a function of risk. For example, a large client expenditure and an ill-defined issue call for cost-plus-fee arrangements, whereas a small client expenditure and a well-defined issue demand a fixed-price arrangement.

EXHIBIT 5-5

Sequence for Contracting

1. Select form of agreement.
2. Draw up contract "shell."
3. Fill out contract.
4. Have attorney verify contract.
5. Obtain consensus from other party.
6. Have both parties sign.

The ownership of the contract is a function of the organization's size and sector. A consultant usually uses a client contract for large organizations in the private (profit or nonprofit) or public sector. However, for medium-size or small clients, the consultant normally uses a consultant contract.

Draw up a *contract "shell."* All service agreements contain common components, as illustrated 'in Exhibit 5-7. The order may vary depending on the situation, but all of these elements must be included to make the document legal. The "shell" is a standard form that can be filled in with the particulars of your services. In some instances, clients will request that you use their contracts. Nonetheless, it is sound practice to be familiar with the parts of a contract and have one ready.

EXHIBIT 5-6

Various Payment Schemes for Consulting Contracts

Name	*Definition*	*Use*
Retainer	A fee paid per unit of time for services on an "on-call" arrangement.	Usually a letter agreement. Consultant provides specific services to client on an ongoing basis and is paid a minimal amount each time period (week or month) to be available for such service provision.
Time and material	Client pays consultant a lump sum fee for actual hours and materials used in providing services.	This is a per diem arrangement with consultant rates decided on in advance. A letter agreement or formal contract signifies the fixed duration over which this holds.
Cost plus fee	Consultant receives reimbursement for all direct and indirect costs incurred plus a "profit" fee. Allowance is made for client payment of over-budget costs.	This is a formal contract arrangement, which is usually made with a large company or public sector client, to resolve an issue that is not defined precisely. Consultant assumes minimal risk but may make minimal profit.

Fixed price	A contractual obligation in which the consultant receives a set fee for performing tasks independent of any contingencies or cost increases. The fee includes all costs and profit.	Used when client issue is well defined. Consultant assumes risk here, but if completed assignment is under budget, he or she can make a large profit. Generally used with a large company or public sector client.
Variations	Fee as percentage of client sales, income plus fee plus expenses, cost plus incentive fee, etc.	Used in various situations to provide added inducement for consultant to complete assignment expediently. Not a contingency arrangement.

EXHIBIT 5-7

Elements of a Consulting Contract

Preamble
Sets forth the mutual intention and purpose of consultant and client in undertaking the consulting assignment.

Consultant Tasks
Describes the various effects of the consultant and the expected operating practices.

Client Tasks
Designates the various efforts that the client is responsible for

Special Conditions
Delimits the contingencies and changes to the contract, and provides for termination, liability, disputes, copyrights, and any additional concerns.

Payment of Consultant's Fee
Spells out exact terms and conditions of payment for tasks stated above.

Execution
Shows binding nature of agreement, observance of statutes, and asks for consultant and client signatures.

Fill out the contract. Now the relevant sections of your proposal are matched or referenced in the contract. Any special conditions are stated, payment mechanisms are specified, and contingencies are added. A fundamental rule of thumb is: *take nothing for granted.* That is, when in doubt, write it out. The contract need not become overly cumbersome, but it should articulate the mutual best interest of client and consultant. Exhibit 5-8 is a sample of

---

EXHIBIT 5-8

Agreement for Consulting Services

Preamble

This agreement entered into this Wednesday, the ninth of February, 1983, by and between:

1. Easy ware, Inc., 113 Productive Blvd., Dayton, Ohio, (513)842-9967, hereinafter referred to as the Client.
2. Syner-Think, Inc., 842 Executive Blvd., Rockville, Maryland, (301)423-5432, hereinafter referred to as the Consultant.

Witnesseth, whereas the Client and the Consultant wish to enter into an agreement for the purpose of developing a mail-order marketing strategy. Now, therefore, it is mutually agreed that the following objectives will be carried out, including:

• Assessment of marketing strategies
• Mail-order counseling
• Implementation of mail-order cataloguing

Consultant Tasks

The work effort detailed below is based on the assignment proposal, No. CS-0034, submitted by the Consultant to the Client on November 20, 1982. Appropriate reference should be made to this document, included as Appendix A. Time frame, costs, tasks, and management of proposal No. CS- 0034 apply herein.

A. The Consultant shall:
   • Examine the current marketing techniques of EASYWARE, INC. to ascertain problem areas,
   • Develop basic methods for improving the marketing efforts, o Assess the potential for mail-order marketing of EASY WARE's home care products division,

- Develop a catalogue for mail orders and implement a marketing strategy based on the assessment.
- Maintain the results of the mail-order marketing, and generate a maintenance procedure for future sales,
- Administer all aspects of the contract.

B. The Consultant will regularly communicate with the designated Client representatives in reviewing and evaluating the progress to date. Working Closely, both parties will effectively implement the agreed- upon marketing changes. Further, the effort of the Consultant is nonassignable.

C. The Consultant will furnish to the Client the following deliverables:
- Time Schedule of Tasks: by February 20, 1983.
- Periodic Reports (each month) describing the progress to date.
- A reproducible Draft of the Final Report: by June 20, 1984. This Report will include a characterization of the work performed and a summary of the results produced.

D. The Consultant will prepare an evaluation of the consulting effort and furnish this to the Client for joint discussion

E. The Consultant will employ a computer technician on a subcontract to do marketing data analyses. Also, the Consultant will purchase time in a time-shared mode.

F. The Consultant, employees of Consultant, and subcontractors are not to be considered employees of Client. Further, the Consultant assumes all responsibility for wages, taxes, or other payment required.

G. The Consultant is an independent agent under Contract with the Client to provide services in an objective and expedient manner. All professional ethical standard will be upheld, including but not limited to: the confidentiality of all materials, interviews, analyses, and reports until authorization is given to release any of them; the absence of conflict of interest; the charge of fees commensurate with services performed; and the right to withdraw from the assignment if its conduct is being sorely impaired.

Tasks

The Client shall:
- Appoint a technical and/or management liaison person for the Consultant
- Provide whatever internal records, documents, or data are needed to carry out the consulting tasks.
- Evaluate the consulting effort and share the findings with the Consultant.

- Work closely with the Consultant to ensure that all tasks are done in an expedient and effective manner.

Special Conditions

1. Optional Services: The Consultant shall provide the Client with modified or related services to the tasks stated above only with prior written approval, including means for additional compensation.
2. Contract Changes: This contract shall be amended, extended, or negotiated only with the expressed written consent of both parties. Any changes warranted will take effect no less than thirty (30) days after joint approval.
3. Termination: The contract can be terminated by either party in thirty (30) days after written intent is communicated to the other party. If Client defaults, payment is due Consultant up to the date of termination. IF Consultant defaults, Client payments are made up to the date when notice is given.
4. Liability: Consultant is not liable for any damages or fee penalties if the consulting issue is not resolved. However, through joint agreement, Consultant is liable for an amount not to exceed $20,000, or the fee, whichever is less, for any professional negligence, unethical conduct, injury, death, property damage, or slander to any Client personnel or facility, respectively, during the performance of this contract.

     Arbitration: Any dispute or claim stemming from the execution of services or the payment of fee shall attempt to be resolved in an amicable way by both parties to this Agreement. Failing this, any remaining controversy or dispute in connection with this contract shall be settled by arbitration in accordance with the rules of the American Arbitration Association. The award in any arbitration proceeding shall be final. The judgment thereon may be entered into any court having such jurisdiction on application of either party.

Payment of Consultant's Fee

For accepted performance of the stated contract tasks, Client agrees to compensate Consultant in the following manner:

A. This contract is a performance fee arrangement wherein Consultant is paid full amount of bid plus 3 percent of the before-taxes profit gain of the mail-order marketing activity six months after the mail-order marketing begins.

B. Payments are due to Consultant at the end of every two-month period throughout the duration of the sixteen-month consultant effort. Such invoices are for the preceding two months' work.

C. Client agrees to pay at least $1000 dollars per two months but which shall not exceed $1800 dollars per two months for an accurately itemized invoice due at the beginning of each alternate month. Client agrees to prompt compensation of Consultant, within thirty (30) days of invoice receipt.

D. It is mutually agreed that if Consultant payments become more than thirty (30) days overdue (from time of invoice submitted), a VA percent service charge will be added per week of late Client compensation. If after three invoices, Client account is still past due, Consultant can terminate provision of consulting services. Client is liable for delinquent payments, and a claim can be made by Consultant for past fees plus legal costs.

Execution

This Agreement shall be binding on the parties mentioned for their expressed benefit, and shall be governed by the laws of the State of Executed, in duplicate, this Agreement as of the day and year first above written.

Client (type name of client) By . . . (signature) (typed name and designation of client representative)	Consultant (type name of consultant) By . . . (signature) (typed name and designation of consultant representative)

a completed client/consultant agreement drawn up by the consultant. This formal contract would also apply to a letter agreement, a subcontract, or a multiple-party arrangement. Second, the client at times assumes complete liability for the assignment. This might occur when the client guards the safety of the consultant, assures the risk for a consultant/client inventory, gives permission to use client property, or acts as the prime contractor subcontracting to the consultant.

However, such instances are rare. Nonetheless, the assignment of risk is based on faith and past experience. Third, strict conditions are stated for client failure to pay. The consultant can have a clause under "Termination" stating that early termination for any reason by the client would be subject to a penalty of x thousand dollars. Remember, agreements are both legal documents and a mutual intent to satisfy needs. The client's acceptance of your conditions is related directly to his or her need for your services. The more flexibility the client has in the timing of services and choice of consultants, the less receptive he or she will be to stringent consultant demands. This is discussed further below in the section "Negotiating the Contract."

Review the contract with an attorney. Since a contract is an agreement to provide services for a fee with protection from loss, it is important to seek the advice of a lawyer. Ask the attorney the following questions: Have I done a credible job in securing proper terms for myself? Have I given options or specifications that are in the other party's best interest? Is there anything else I need to add to the agreement? The lawyer will review the contract, suggest modifications or additions, and discuss negotiating strategy.

Obtain consensus from the other party. Next, the contract is given to the client to examine. Encourage the client to make suggestions in order to minimize conflicts or misunderstandings later. Then, negotiate the final terms (as discussed below), verify the contract's completeness, and sign.

Sample Task IV

Obtain a client contract. One way to do this is by asking your local General Services Administration Office for a fixed-price contract form for "support services" provided to the federal government. Next, get a copy of a consultant contract, either your own or a colleague's. Compare the two contracts. What additional obligations would you have contracting with the government-both formal, contractual ones, and informal, procedural ones? Does a more complex agreement ensure greater productivity or more professional work? Why? Finally, make notes showing when it is best to use your contract and when it is best to use the client's. When and why would you persuade a client who wants to use his or her contract to use yours?

NEGOTIATING THE CONTRACT

In a sense, you begin negotiating from the first moment you meet with your would-be client. By the time proposals are reviewed, the candidate selected, and the contracts drawn up, you should have a strong impression of what the client desires-and how to satisfy these desires. The decision to negotiate traditionally rests with the client, since he or she needs information to choose the best candidate. On the other hand, there are additional reasons to negotiate

---

EXHIBIT 5-9

Advantages and Disadvantages to Negotiating

For the Client

Pro
- An effective way to judge candidates.
- A legally-agreed-to method to effectively iron out differences between consultant(s) and client.
- Additional indication to upper management of sincerity in hiring a consultant

Con:
- Another step in contracting that could delay start of work.
- If consultant already chosen, any questions or concerns can be handled informally.
- Policy to do it only for large contracts in terms of dollars, time commitment, or both.

For the Consultant:

Pro:
- Excellent means of demonstrating abilities "under fire," establishing better rapport and convincing client of your competitive edge.
- Provides a forum for increasing opportunity to reach a mutually respected agreement.
- Affords chance to give "a little" to gain "a lot."

Con.
- Too time consuming to prepare for properly, unless negotiating large contract.
- Lack of negotiating skills.
- Has the potential to hurt more than help consultant's position.

(such as contract clarifications, or modifications to the scope of work). Thus, speak up for a negotiating session if one is required. Exhibit 5-9 describes the pros and cons of negotiating.

In addition, Exhibit 5-10 lists some tips that are worth keeping in mind if you do enter into a negotiation. To come out "on top" after a negotiating session, you must know two things: what your priorities are and how much you can compromise regarding the consulting tasks, the contract, or the client relationship. Knowing this information beforehand puts you in a stronger position. Thus, as with any other phase of the consulting assignment, you must be prepared and have the proper attitude.

EXHIBIT 5-10

Tips on Consultant Negotiating

Do	*Don't*
Try to learn precisely what client wants in contract.	Dwell on minor concerns. Create conflict for the sport of it.
Understand why client is negotiating.	Become unduly upset if communication falters. Keep "your cool" and move on.
Watch for responses that indicate how competition stands.	Negotiate cold. Practice with colleagues beforehand.
Negotiate items that are catalysts to establishing better communication.	Play detective or be detected. Present all items that it is necessary to discuss.
Be prepared to yield and to compromise.	Be taken in by client ploys. Stick to agenda and finish it.
Stress strong and weak points of contract and show positive benefits of your completing it.	Be afraid to question client for clarification, assessment, or prognosis.
Couch comments as much as possible in client context.	Make false promises.
	Give away more than you can afford.
	Forget to put outcome of negotiations in writing.
	Negotiate if fundamental contractual promises change by the time you reach the bargaining table.

Sample Task V

Ask a colleague to join you in a mock client bargaining session. Have your associate be the client and you be the consultant. Role-play negotiations prompted by the client. Now do the same for consultant-prompted negotiations. Critique the sessions. How can the consultant role be improved? Finally, reverse roles and simulate another negotiation. Critique this session. Have these sessions helped prepare you for more effective communication with the client? If yes, how? If no, why?

Case Example: Bargaining Down the Drain?

I will reluctantly tell you about one of my negotiating sessions that I would rather forget about. Having been selected by a client to do some survey work on energy-usage patterns, I decided to schedule a meeting to verify the work and payment schedules because I noticed that they were incorrectly diagrammed in the client-generated contract. I phoned the client and suggested a meeting in his office during the lunch hour to correct these errors. He agreed. Upon my arrival, I found nothing short of chaos. The client had failed to mention that lunch hours in his office were a social "free for all "people chatting, playing cards, meditating, or exercising. How were we going to conduct business? Psychologists call this "scene" a do-every thing/do-nothing condition. After about 30 minutes, I had enough. I squeezed in words to the effect that I would make another appointment to complete this contract. After four tries and no luck-you guessed it-I chalked the encounter up to experience.

SPECIAL TOPIC: AVOIDING FREE BUSINESS

In any situation lies the seed of something for nothing. A client wants to hire you to fulfill a set of specified tasks. In return, a certain payment will be made for doing these tasks. Yet, if your proposal or the contract are not properly written, the client could walk away with a "how to" and not need your assistance.

To avoid any situation of this sort, keep the following pointers in mind:

Write a results-oriented proposal. Sketch the procedures, tools, or methods to be used. Focus on the outcomes, the applications, and the benefits. The client's main interest is the end result, independent of how you got there. Be safe-have him or her pay to see you get there.

Avoid informal favors. At times, a client may say, "Well, since you've done such a fine job thus far with project A, why don't you take a look at project B?" If B costs little compared to the contract revenue, some consultants will do it gratis to enhance their rapport with the client. Still, this practice, if repeated, can lead to your shortchanging your effort by spending too much time on noncontracted tasks and thereby decreasing the revenue from contracted tasks. Incorporate a clause in your contract for modifying the scope of work. And then as additions or changes arise, you can simply let the client know you can do them, but at an additional charge. The decision is up to the client but remember that your services are procured through payment.

Handle follow-up requests carefully. Once the initial contract is terminated, future work becomes a primary concern to some clients. Many times, they will ask you to assist them with a crisis by giving advice over the telephone or in a short visit. Such a practice can become habit forming. This habit is a bad one only if you do not receive compensation for this "free-lance" advice. One means of doing so would be to negotiate a retainer contract (as discussed above) with the client. If for some reason this arrangement is not mutually suitable, you can send the client a bill each month for any services rendered. Consulting for free creates dependency and produces lower-quality results. Let's be fair; services should be exchanged only for payment.

SUMMARY AND EXTENSION

Few books teach effective contracting; thus most consultants, with or without a lawyer, muddle through the drawing up of standard agreements. Performing services for the client means providing accurate, fair, and comprehensible work. To do this, you must also be on top of the contract provisions and arrangements, ensuring that they are what you want. There's nothing wrong with being shrewd in drawing up a contract. Bid or no bid, the client should feel that you made the right choice. Deciding to go ahead implies a proposal written cogently, creatively, and accurately. Defending your ideas, experience, and ability presents an opportunity to convince the client that the assignment will turn out well. The material is "deaf" as long as no one is listening. Consider it wisely, for you can get the work as long as you put forth the effort.

Chapter Six

Carrying Out the Consulting Engagement

SNAPSHOT

This chapter describes the object of any consulting experience-the services provided. We examine the process through which the services are rendered, the various steps of a consulting assignment, the various roles a consultant assumes, and the responsibilities of both client and consultant. We conclude the chapter by demonstrating how to manage an engagement effectively.

Case Example 6-1: To Serve or to Swerve

Anne S., a colleague of mine, recounted the following story. Her client, company A, asked her to find out how its contracts with suppliers were negotiated. Anne wrote up a proposal, including a precise set of tasks designed to reform the contracting and negotiating procedure. The client accepted the proposal eagerly. After several weeks of observation and analysis, Anne produced a written report that criticized the current contractual procedures and documents, but also offered several realistic recommendations for correcting the faulty practices. The client disliked the presentation, the findings, and the implications for the company. "Company A was furious," Anne told me. "The thought of reforming a contract or its use was unthinkable. They expected to gain more sales by doing the same thing with only slight changes." Anne was terminated and paid four months later for her time.

Unfortunately, this situation occurs frequently due to ignorance and miscommunication. This chapter demonstrates how to provide consulting services wisely and sensitively.

EXHIBIT 6-1

Elements Required for a Consultation

Element	*Description*	*Characteristic*
Service	Any combination of advice, procedures, and outputs to complete a consulting assignment.	Depends on the specifications of the contract and the consultant's skills.
Provision	The means to fulfill the service.	Variable. Depends on service description.
Consulting mode	The method chosen to carry out the consulting assignment.	Generally, behavorial, technical, or combined modes.
Client organization	The setting in which the consulting occurs.	The consultation begins and ends here.
Issue	The problem confronting the client in the client organization.	Catalyst for the consultation and the objective is to resolve it.
Process	The generic sequence of steps to carry out a consulting assignment.	Done by most consultants concerned with effecting change in the client organization.

LEARNING THE BASICS

The primary myth attached to the practice of consulting is that anyone can do it. No prior training, no awareness, no understanding of concepts and skills are required. Instead, limited exposure to the specific expertise of various business or professional people and a desire to package this expertise and sell it to clients are enough to become a successful consultant-so the myth goes. However, the key to a successful consultation is in knowing the service elements, the participants, and the process that links the two together. Exhibit 6-1 lists the elements in a consultation performed by the people identified in Exhibit 6-2. Together, these exhibits define consulting-the

---

EXHIBIT 6-2

Persons Involved in the Consultation

Person	*Description*	*Comments*
Client	Holds a decision-making position in an organization. Generally, responsible for hiring and implementing the services of consultants.	Most consultants work for two clients: the main contact and the head(s) of the organization.
Client group	The peers or subordinates who are directly or peripherally related to the consultation.	There is a web of communication necessary to execute a consulting assignment effectively.
Consultant	The person or team performing the consultation. The leader is responsible for establishing a client relationship and completing the assignment.	There can also be part-time consultants, consultant advisors, and internal consultants assisting the primary consultant.

---

process by which a consultant seeks to resolve an issue within a client organization.

By itself, however, the definition is incomplete; for consulting involves the active participation of parties to resolve an issue in a timely and effective way. Thus the definition is tied to a generic process, which contains the following characteristics:

General application. The process can be used for any type of client in the United States or abroad, regardless of the contractual and management methods specified.

Flexibility. Each assignment is defined by using some or all of the process steps. (For completeness, the entire process is shown here.)

Responsibility. Client and consultant share joint responsibility to effect change in the client organization. Such change is made in a professional manner based on mutual trust and respect.

Exhibit 6-3 briefly describes each step in the consulting process. Many consultants view consulting as a bag of tricks, a secret technique, or a remedy. And many clients view it as some type of black box spurting out results

EXHIBIT 6-3

Steps in the Consulting Assignment

Step	*Description*	*Implication*
Recognizing the issue	Issued recognized by client. Measures tried to resolve issue. Decision made to use consultant.	Client establishes systematic procedures to tackle issue.
Finding the right consultant	Several consultants contacted and inter viewed. Proposals solicited and evaluted. Consultant selected and contract secured.	Consultant can also make initial contact. Consultant can also receive sole-source award.
Starting the assignment	Client and consultant refine assignment. Consultant becomes more familiar with client organization. Client/consultant establish relationship.	Consultant transmits techniques on how each task can be accomplished.
Defining the issue	Consultant discovers underlying causes to issue. Client and consultant arrive at consensus of what true issue is.	Consultant uses data-gathering techniques to find and verify cases.
Finding means to resolve the issue	Consultant produces various feasible alternatives for handling issue. Client and consultant form decision frame work. Client chooses most suitable alternative.	Method of discovery varies with issue.

Implement-ing the chosen alternative	Consultant develops implementation plan and receives client approval. Consultant prepares to cope with client or client group resistance to change.	Consultant must ensure that plan has performance controls and can be modified. Consultant uses one or more techniques to engender client acceptance of changes.
Monitoring the resolution	Consultant implements resolution. Consultant works through barriers to change. Consultant submits report and client reviews it.	If written documentation is necessary, consultant uses techniques similar to those used in proposal writing.
Evaluating and terminating the assignment	Consultant and client each evaluate consulting activity Joint client/consultant evaluation occurs. Contract is completed.	Is generally not done. Is new innovation in consulting assignment.
Follow-on consulting	Consultant and client discuss future consultant input. Consultant determines potential for new assignments.	Client feels able to handle similar issue in the future.

that can be used immediately. Exhibit 6-3 corrects this picture. Further, consulting skills are the means to carry out this process. Such skills require the following:

- The ability to obtain accurate and relevant facts to support the issue definition and resolution steps. The capacity to search for all causes of the problem and to formulate alternative solutions with the short- and long-term consequences in mind. The sensitivity to root out the real issue and to discuss it openly and honestly with the client.
- The understanding to realize that no resolution is perfect and that the real challenge begins at the implementation stage. (See Exhibit 6-4 for required skills.)

EXHIBIT 6-4

Consulting Skills

Process Step	*Skills*
Finding the right consultant	Initial marketing to client Organization and writing a proposal Use of contracts
Starting the assignment	Consensus building Diplomacy
Defining the issue	Data-gathering techniques Listening tools Giving and receiving feedback
Means to resolve issue	Generation of alternatives Decision methods Conducting a meeting
Implementing the chosen alternative	Implementation planning Conflict resolution Overcoming resistance to change
Monitoring the resolution	Control techniques Report writing
Evaluation and terminating assignment	Consultant evaluation Client evaluation Joint evaluation
Follow-on consulting	Determining future arrangements

The implications of these skills are:

1. These techniques are required for a successful consulting engagement independent of the subject area(s) and of the problem(s).
2. No solution to a proficient consulting assignment is "canned." A consulting project's success depends on the support and understanding of the client.
3. Problem solving is normally done within a disciplinary area-education, economics, engineering, accounting, psychology, management, physics-but consulting skills are learned on the job.
4. An evaluation provides an opportunity to learn how to improve the delivery of services, as well as to sustain client rapport for future activities.

The interpersonal skills-writing a proposal and a final report, conducting a meeting, giving and receiving feedback, overcoming resistance to change and resolving conflicts-needed to practice consulting effectively and the problem-solving skills-defining a client issue, data-gathering techniques, generation of alternatives, decision methods, implementation planning, and assignment evaluation-are presented in greater detail in another recent book by the author, *Principles and Practices of Professional Consulting,* published by Bermont Books, Washington, D.C., 1982.

ADMINISTERING THE ENGAGEMENT

The satisfaction and accomplishment of a consulting assignment lies with helping a client solve problem(s). Yet the value of any approach or perspective depends on how well it is communicated and understood. Communication combines a consultant's organizing and directing skills.

Poor management and ineffective use of these skills can sorely hamper the success of any engagement.

Specifically, we are talking about the following controls:

Means to ensure that deadlines are kept
Methods for recording all effort expended
Means to ensure regular communication with the client
Method to sense unrecognized concerns before they hamper consulting services

Exhibits 6-5 through 6-8 demonstrate how to apply these controls. Exhibit 6-5 is a planning tool for the consultant, letting you know what deliverables are due, what items are used to organize an engagement, and how a project

---

EXHIBIT 6-5

Documents for a Consulting Engagement

Item	*Source*	*Application*
Proposal	Discussions with client Data references Past experience	To secure consulting assignment
Contract	Client's from consultant's from combination	To establish professional working relationship
Milestone chart	PERT critical Path Gantt chart	To specify the deadlines and deliverables
Progress Report	Work log preliminary result	To inform client periodically of consultant's accomplishments
Final Report	Progress reports Engagement results and implementation	To describe and summarize the outcome of the consultation
Supportive material	Varied	To enhance the client's Problem solving in the future

---

EXHIBIT 6-6

Milestone Chart

Project *Computer Selection*
Client *Ajax Affiliates*

Month

Tasks	Jan.	Feb.	Mar.	Apr.	May	June
1. Sign contract	___					
2. Assess client's data-processing activities and needs	___					
3. Develop preliminary means to satisfy task 2		___				
4. Client chooses means to automate			___			
5. Present several alternative computer systems			___			
6. Assist client with evaluation process				___		
7. Install selected system				___		
8. Make enhancements and document effort					___	
9. Present Final Report for review and critique						___

Note: Progress Reports are given monthly.

---

flows from idea to finished product. By contrast, Exhibit 6-6 specifies the what and when of any engagement, leaving no doubt in the client's mind as to the sequence of consulting activities. Also, this chart restates the work tasks given in the contract (Chapter Five) with dates of completion. Exhibit 6-7 is an "internal" device used by the consultant to record effort expended as it happens. This device gives the raw data used in the Progress Report and tabulates, for billing purposes, the time expended. In addition, it monitors how well the consultant tasks are performed, and it helps to uncover snags, delays, and unexpected constraints to the effort. Also, this work sheet records minor modifications to the order or outcome of the specified tasks.

It can assist the consultant in spotting unexpected changes to the engagement. Finally, Exhibit 6-8 shows what elements comprise a Progress Report, a document that provides regular communication between client and

EXHIBIT 6-7

Work Log

Project Computer selection	Client Ajax Affiliates		Date Week of February 4	
Day	*Item*	*Time*	*Result*	*Note*
Tuesday, Feb.1	Hardware configuration analysis	4.2 hours	Mostly mainframe poorly connected peripheral system	Met with Jane Allison, data Processing manager Need review Service Contracts
Thursday, Feb. 3	Information gathering On alternative hardware	3.6 hours	Have cost data on alternative processors	Find compatible peripheral equipment
Friday, Feb. 4	(1) Do Progress report	0.45 hours	Ready for client on Feb 8	
	(2) Contact colleagues and discuss computer system designs	2.1 hours	Ready to present three approaches to client	Contact favored Suppliers to get system price quotes
	(3) write up method used in developing alternative system designs	1.7 hours		Present at Feb 15 meeting

Total hours, week of February 4:	12.05 hours

consultant and summarizes effort to date. In total, these four exhibits plus the Contract and Financial Report provide the consultant with an effective guide to execute the consulting assignment.

SPECIAL TOPIC: USING A COMPUTER SENSIBLY

Most consulting assignments entail collecting and evaluating data, making presentations and writing reports-three good reasons for using a computer. However, a computer is a tool designed for certain repetitive operations and not for unique, abstract activities. So if you think your consulting task involves the use of a computer, ask yourself these questions:

- How often will I require information processing?
- Am I capable of performing these data manipulation tasks myself, or should someone else do them?
- Can I earn additional income by selling computer services?
- The answers to these questions will help you decide whether you should buy or lease a computer, or hire someone else to do your computer work.

EXHIBIT 6-8

Progress Report

	Project *Computer Selection*
Section	Client *Ajax Affiliates*
I. Summary of Project Scope	Time *Month of January*
II. Over view of Effort to Date	
III. Detailed Description of Activities	
IV. Special Concerns and Contingencies	
V. Projected Effort	
VI. Invoice	
VII. Supporting Information	

In any case, there are several pointers to keep in mind:

- The more you can define the tasks, the more cost effective any computer use will be.
- A computer system should be selected, first, based on the match of software features to your information requirements, and then on which hardware can best operate the chosen software.
- Automation activities are based on efficient data collection and entry procedures.
- Successful use of a computer system requires skill, insight, and ingenuity.

SUMMARY AND EXTENSION

This chapter succinctly describes the knowledge required to carry out a consulting assignment successfully. Providing services requires skills defining and resolving client issues, and fostering and deepening client rapport, respect, and trust. The goal of any assignment is for the client, independently, to tackle similar issues in the future. In addition, the consultant will move on to other assignments. A primary source for future consulting is a satisfied client. However, other avenues are also available to expand your practice. In the next chapter we present ways to discover such sources through advertising and promotion.

Chapter Seven

Using Advertising and Promotion Effectively

SNAPSHOT

To practice consulting, you need three things: a client problem, skills in problem solving, and a means of bringing the two together. After solving the critical problem, the consultant then moves ahead to asking: What other client problems are of interest? What future additional skills are required? What further means exist to find such clients? This chapter answers the last question. Even though advertising and promotion techniques do provide avenues (not otherwise known or open) to discovering contracts, they are not substitutes for marketing methods (discussed in Chapter Four). Advertising and promotion provide new and different ways to learn and communicate about consulting, *and* they can also be channels for earning extra revenue. Still, advertising and promotion make sense only if the consultant is ready to broaden his or her contacts and experiences in the consulting environment. Without motivation, the techniques presented herein will be at best, under-used, and, at worst, wasted.

REDEFINING ADVERTISING AND PROMOTION

Consulting is not done primarily to sell products, but to provide services. As such, advertising and promotion are used not only for sales but to transfer information and improve operations. Advertising is the direct publicity of consulting services through one or more communication media. It is the means by which information about such services is transferred to a general audience over prepaid communication channels. A consultant's ad should be brief, provocative, descriptive, and appeal to a broad range of clients.

Examples of advertising include the brochure, business card, pitch, or brief notice. Examples of advertising media include direct mail, handout, telephone solicitation, newspaper, radio, television, journal, newsletter, or trade publication. The result is to generate client interest in buying the services portrayed.

Promotion, on the other hand, is more flexible. It is the indirect publicity of consulting services, usually over one communication medium at a time. The intended audience is a specific group or market segment.

There are two kinds of promotion: primary and secondary.

Primary promotion activities signify or enhance the consultant's professional reputation, but usually accrue no income-or income only to pay for expenses. Examples include articles in trade, professional, or academic journals; letters to the editor of newspapers; lectures to business, community, or professional groups; a syndicated news column in a newsletter or newspaper; television or radio talk show appearances; book reviews; press releases; a directory listing; attendance at a business, regulatory, or other public meeting; active membership in a professional association; and so on. From the message brought forth, respective attenders, listeners, readers, or reviewers could request more information about services or pass along the consultant's name to a prospective colleague.

Secondary promotion is the development of service packets that are sold for income. Generally, these packets are an outgrowth of the primary services provided to individual clients. They serve the new clients by appealing to a wider audience than the independent consultant can service one on one. The revenue obtained is used to improve the quality of services provided, as well as to augment the advertising and promotion campaigns.

Examples include self-published newsletters or books, client-oriented courses or seminars, correspondence courses, educational media (cassette tapes, films, TV programs, surveyor testing tools), or standardized service instruments (that is, for marketing research, regulation enforcement, program evaluation, decision making, and so on). There is no fixed number of advertising or promotional techniques that you can use. To choose the appropriate method for your needs, consider the following:

Ability. Not all consultants can or should advertise in every type of medium. Decide which method uses your abilities to their best advantage.

Time. How much time should you spend on advertising or promotion? The minimum amount that it takes to achieve results. This does not imply skimping on time, but rather, deciding which methods will work given your ability and time constraints.

Cost. Since the cost of the different techniques varies, pick those that will show zero or positive return initially. Later, as the business grows, you can afford a negative cash flow, since it will be more than compensated for by new client engagements.

Client market. Different advertising and promotional techniques have distinct effects on a client's willingness to buy. One way to discover which method works best is to rank the techniques in terms of positive client buying power. Then test the client market and correct your list as the data come in.

Sample Task I

List all the advertising and promotion techniques you have used as a consultant. List all the techniques that you would like to use. Are the lists different? Why?

EXPLORING WAYS TO ADVERTISE

How do you mount a successful advertising campaign? Objective factors, such as time, money, and ability, as well as subjective factors, such as creativity and contacts, determine your campaign's outcome. No two campaigns are alike, nor is one better than the other. You can be as creative as you wish as long as business is stimulated. Exhibit 7-1 describes the elements in an advertisement. Exhibit 7-2 lists the various types of advertising with the respective media. Let's look individually at each method described in Exhibit 7-2.

EXHIBIT 7-1

Elements of an Advertisement

1. Frequency: the number of times the ad appears
2. Time frame: specific date and time of advertisement
3. Size: the amount of space or time it takes to present the ad
4. Message: basic information given to the client
5. Medium: the way your message is presented: written, oral, or mixed?
6. Price: the unit cost of producing each ad
7. Fee: the charge for placing the ad
8. Expected return: the new business/expense ratio for the ad
9. Placement: where the ad will be placed: for example, in the front or back of newspaper, on one or more TV stations, or in the same location in each monthly issue of a newsletter

---

EXHIBIT 7-2

Scope of Advertising

Method	*Medium*
Brochure	Newspaper
Brochure	Journal
Telephone solicitation	Television
Announcement	Yellow Pages
Commercial	Newsletter
	Trade publication
	Consultant brokerage
	Direct mail
	Public places (buildings, transit, billboards, etc.)

Brochure. As described in Chapter Four, the brochure is the consultant's basic marketing tool. It can also be sent to a large number of prospective clients to advertise your services (see Exhibit 7-3). The more current and accurate your data are, the better the chances are for a response. Second, sending prospective clients a brochure is an inexpensive way to make an initial contact. However, the average response for bulk mailing is low-around 2 percent-and many respondents turn out to be poor candidates for consulting services. In addition, the client is first not given an opportunity to meet you in person or talk with you on the telephone. A sounder approach is to study mailing lists, directories, conference attendance sheets, and client advertisements, then select clients to contact by telephone. After the calls, follow up with a mailing. The contacts are smaller, but the chances of securing contracts are greater.

Announcement. An announcement, a written description of your services, is placed in a newspaper, journal, trade publication, or newsletter. The format may vary, but all the elements in Exhibits 7-1 and 7-3 must be considered. Exhibit 7-4, an announcement for data-base management consultants, is rather long and would probably appear in the advertising sections of a computer newspaper, newsletter, or journal. The ad's frequency and time frame are tied directly to the publication's schedule.

The ad's effectiveness can be determined only by analyzing the results and testing the ad in other markets.

Commercial. This form of advertising is rarely used by consultants because it is extremely expensive. If you are interested in running a radio or television

EXHIBIT 7-3

Advertising Techniques

Technique	Use	Resource	Contact Examples
Brochure	Cain client entry	Direct mail list	Standard Rate and Data Services, Skokie, Illinois
		Associations	National Trade and Professional Associations Book Encyclopedia of Associations
		Client Name	Standard & Poor's Moody's Federal Yellow Pages Consultants and Consulting Associations Association conference attendance sheets Client advertisements
Announcement	Present services through paid advertisement	Newspaper Magazine Journal Newsletter	Wall Street Journal
			Business Week Consulting Opportunities Journal The Professional Consultant Public service announcement
Commercial	Communicate directly over the airwaves	Radio	Standard commercial,
Consultant brokerage	Consultant pays finder's fee for assignments	Television Firm	Consultant brokerage Mt. View, CA 94040 Consultant's Clearinghouse, McLean, VA 22101

EXHIBIT 7-4

Consulting Advertisement

Hear Ye! Hear Ye!

Have you wondered why Data Base Management Systems (DBMS) are ever more costly?

Have you noticed how un wieldly they've become?

Have you considered changing DBMS, but felt as if you had a rope around your neck?

If any of these questions apply to you, BASYC SISTEMS, INC., offers a way out

If more efficient and cost-effective data management is your goal, BASYC SISTEMS, INC., can help ensure your success

If special configurations are a concern, BASYC SISTEMS, INC., can handle all conversion and emulation problems.

We're not soft on innovation. We are long on solving your particular problem. For consultants who correct system deficiencies in an individual way, contact

Jerry Automate, V.P

BSI   New Business Development

400 Byte Boulevard

Houston, TX 77056

or phone   (800) 444-3325

---

commercial, follow the criteria described in Exhibit 7-1. To overcome the high cost, you might run a commercial with other independent consultants or professional associations.

Advertising consulting services are relatively new, and a longer discussion of the ethics involved is taken up in Chapter Nine. Here, it is important to note that advertising is a supplementary tool; it has little effect on building your reputation. Once your reputation is established, advertising can enhance your sales potential. Promotion can accomplish the same thing, as we will discover below.

Sample Task II

Put your brochure in front of you. Imagine that your business exceeds $1 million in sales this year. How would you change your brochure? Why?

Take the new brochure and create a full-page ad for the *New York Times.* How would you alter the ad if it appeared in *Chemical and Engineering News,* in *Science,* or in *Foreign Affairs?* Writing for an audience can make a significant difference in your advertising campaign.

PROMOTING YOUR SERVICES

One way to view promotion is to say that a consultant is always promoting his or her services. However, Exhibits 7-5 and 7-6 present some specific methods you might use.

Brief articles. Publishing an article in a desirable periodical is an excellent way to attract clients. First, choose the appropriate periodical.

Survey the journals and magazines that you receive; then, examine copies of other journals in your field. The following resource books are also extremely helpful: *The Directory of Publishing Opportunities in Journals and Periodicals, The National Directory of Newsletters, Literary Marketplace (LMP),* and *Business Publications: Rates and Data.*

Pick out at least five publications that might print your perspectives and insights. Find out the requirements for publication: length, format, bibliography, and review procedures. Also, determine how often each one is published and the size of readership. Follow the publication's guidelines and submit the article for review. A timely, well-written piece that mirrors the publication's objectives is likely to be accepted. Writing an article also presents you with an opportunity to increase your skills and knowledge.

Enclose with your article a brief biographical sketch and a press photo. Many periodicals and professional journals also feature book reviews.

Reviewing current titles is an excellent way to communicate with other consultants as well as with interested clients.

Be sure that any time you make a contact, you include a brochure. As your business grows, modify the brochure. You may want to have different brochures for different clients or different services. As your business expands, so will your capabilities, which should be reflected in your brochure.

Sample Task III

Come up with an idea for a short article that you would like to publish. Write an outline. Who constitutes the intended audience? What contribution will your article make? Why? How can writing this piece augment your business. Would you be better off writing something else?

EXHIBIT 7-5

Primary Promotion Methods

Type	*Media*
1. Short written pieces	
a. Articles	a. Newsletter, trade periodical, magazine, journal
b. Letters to the editor	b. Newspaper, journal, magazine
c. Editorials	c. Newspaper, journal, newsletter, magazine
d. News clips/stories	d. Newspaper, journal, trade periodical, magazine
e. Press release	e. News services
f. Book review	f. Newsletter, journal, or trade periodical
g. Brochure	g. Handout or mailing
2. Longer written pieces	
a. Book	a. Book publisher or self-publishing
b. Series of articles	b. Journal, newsletter, or trade periodical
c. Syndicated news column	c. Newspaper, newsletter
3. Listing	
a. In association	a. Membership directory
b. Consultants' compendium	b. Business directories
4. Short oral presentation	
A. Speech	A. Public groups, conventions, conferences, and professional affairs
B. Lecture	B. Professional societies, client groups, conferences, and convocations
C. Talk-show appearance	C. Television and radio
5. Longer oral presentation	
a. Testimony	a. Public or private hearing, courtroom proceeding, business meeting, regulatory meeting
b. Academic course	b. Regular university curriculum, university continuing education, trade schools, or vocational certificate programs
6. Miscellaneous	
a . Professional activities	a. Professional organizations
b. Special events	b. Various clients or other consultants

EXHIBIT 7-6

Secondary Promotion Methods

Type	*Media*
1. Written material	
a. Books	a. Self-published
b. Newsletter	b. Self-published
c. Periodicals	c. Group-published
2. Training	
a. In-house courses	a. Client organizations
b. Seminars	b. Publicly sponsored
c. Correspondence course	c. Purchased materials
3. Standardized service instruments	
a. Education	a. Cassette tape, film, TV program, and course guide
b. Technical	b. Procedure format, survey form. computer algorithm, etc.
c. Consulting tools	c. Combination of a or b

Books. These projects are undertaken by consultants who want to write and who are interested in both the short-term and long-term rewards of their efforts: for instance, achieving professional competency. Since few consultants participate in professional activities and certification, well-written books are highly regarded. Researching and synthesizing new information and turning out high-quality written work is a way to improve your skills. Few consultants ever lived on royalties from such efforts, but you can discover new ways to market your skills.

If you are so inclined, here is a brief guide to publishing. First, look at *Book Publisher Directory, Writers' Market, or Literary Marketplace (LMP)*.

Find those publishers who have published books in your subject areas. Call up each publisher and speak to the head of the relevant division. Explain your concept or proposal. If the response is positive, forward your prospectus and outline for consideration. A phone call first is a timesaver and a fast means of finding the right contact. Send enough materials so that the potential publisher can understand your purpose, the book's potential market, and the book's structure and length. Be prepared for rejections and to circulate the book "package" to a number of publishing houses.

Listing. The independent consultant can have his or her name, firm name, address, phone, and areas of service listed in directories. Wasserman's *Consultants and Consulting Organizations,* published by Gale Research Company in Detroit, is a national directory; the *Yellow Pages* in your metropolitan area and the Chamber of Commerce business guide are good local listings. Look for other directories in your special field of interest. If you join professional or trade associations, you can be listed in their membership directories.

Short oral presentations. Speaking engagements include television or radio appearances, or lecturing. The first two are for consultants who have a flair for words and performing. Such events can be fun, but unless they are heard by possible clients, they generally do not generate contracts. On the other hand, delivering well-focused, pertinent lectures to professional groups can be an excellent source of client engagements. Judicious preparation and presentation are the keys to attracting new clients. Ways to make contacts for these events include personal and professional associates who work with or know people in the media, at universities, or at trade or professional associations. Making an entry here is identical to doing so with new clients (Chapter Four). Also, cold-calls on representatives of various professional groups could be equally fruitful since they are in the market for stimulating information for their membership. Contacts can be found in the *Encyclopedia of Associations, Business Organizations and Agencies Directory,* or *Writer's Market.* The public announcements section of the metropolitan or local newspaper is an excellent source of speaking opportunities. Also, holding a press conference can demonstrate your ability to present an issue, handle public feedback~ and show professional concern.

Sample Task IV

Imagine that Tom Brokaw calls you and asks you to be interviewed on the state of consulting in 2009. The taping is in two weeks. How would you respond? Why? If you decide to go ahead with the interview, how would you prepare for it? What ideas would you stress? What image would you wish to convey? How would you this experience be different if you made the contact first? Finally, would you prefer Brokaw to Phil Donahue or Johnny Carson? Why?

Longer oral presentations. Here you provide valuable information to individuals concerned with issues and/or career advancement. For instance, in giving testimony in a court of law, the consultant wears an adversary hat. You are called on to provide unbiased, structured data and analysis to augment the due process of a civil or sometimes a criminal matter. You are being called upon to act as an expert. The testimony is either given for free or done for a client on a retainer. Some firms specialize in adversary consulting. On the other hand, participating in civic, public, or technical hearings as a volunteer enhances your professional standing. In addition, hearings or meetings are suitable places for meeting prospective clients. Such events are normally listed in newspapers, or less frequently in trade or technical publications. Another area of communication is teaching. There are more free-lance consultants practicing today than ever before, yet there are few places where educational instruction is given. The demand for consulting courses often centers on graduate programs in business, engineering, education, or psychology. The courses could focus either on learning the principles and practices of consulting, or the applications and techniques of these principles to specific fields. Another fruitful arena for instruction is adult or continuing education. Most of these programs are affiliated with universities or trade schools. First contact the dean of the continuing education program at your local university or trade school, then propose teaching a course.

Sample Task V

Put together a syllabus for a course on consulting. What elements would it contain? What objectives are you and the students attempting to achieve?

What teaching style will you use? How will you measure the students' performance? Will you include a course evaluation? How will you follow up in terms of potential client contact? Now, formulate a way to sell this course to a university. What are the strong and weak points in your tactic? Will you carry this out?

Miscellaneous. Included in this section are two closely related areas: professional activities and special events. One way to improve your communication skills is to become an active member in a professional organization. Special events-conventions, conferences, and lectures also provide you with an excellent opportunity to expand your network of contacts and work on your interpersonal skills. Check your local community newspaper and association newsletter for listings of events. Another way in which consultants promote their services is by creating and selling products-be they educational devices, technical instruments, or consulting tools. Successfully marketing such items depends on the product, its price, and its market potential. But the basic decision is: Do you want to be in the service *and* product business? That answer depends on what you have to sell, your desire to do so, and the effects of selling on your consulting practice. Two helpful guides to assist you in reaching a decision are Howard L. Shenson's *The Consultant and Productization* and David J. Luck's *Marketing Strategies and Plans.*

Sample Task VI

Choose a consulting product you wish to develop. Describe the product, target the buyers, estimate the cost and price, and state the marketing strategy. How

will you advertise and promote the product? Why? How will your marketing method be similar to and different from your advertising and promotion?
How will marketing the product improve the delivery of your services?

Case Example 1: The Owl and the Shrew

Not long ago, I found out about a consulting firm that provides public relations services to consultants. The firm, CONSULT: P.R., comes into an
organization and assesses the needs for effective advertising and promotion,
sets up a customized program, and then monitors the resulting new sales and
contacts. CONSULT: P.R.'s modus operandi is a short-term profit and quick
reputation. They guarantee three new sales within 90 days after the installa-
tion of their program or half the client's money back.

TYME-WIZE, INC., a new consulting firm, called CONSULT: P.R. about
two months ago, requesting their services.

TYME-WIZE provides performance standards and quality control evaluations for engineering projects. After surveying the firm, CONSULT:P.R.
recommended that it adopt a vigorous "visual" promotion campaign, flooding
the engineering community with ads in newspapers, professional journals,
television, and radio.

The next month TYME-WIZE, INC. ads appeared everywhere.
CONSULT;P.R. recommended how to turn the inquiries into contact meetings. Two weeks of phone calls and letters were acted upon. The blitz continued for a second month. More calls, more leads, and even a few meetings
occurred. At the start of the third month, both firms sat down to review the
current situation: out of 150 responses, there was one lead, zero prospects,
and zero sales. Why did this happen? CONSULT: P.R. had mounted a frenetic
publicity scheme for an inertia-bound industry. They misjudged the engineering market and mismanaged advertising and promotion resources. Engineering firms are slow to use new firms; they prefer to stick with companies with
a proven track record. However, there is a way out for TYMEWIZE, INC.
They should start small: make contacts at a few engineering firms, visit the
firms, attend conferences, and increase their network. It might take a few
meetings before a sale is made. But for now, the time is worth it.

SPECIAL TOPIC: DESCRIBING YOUR CONSULTING IMAGE

Most consultants, like most business people, think of image in concrete
terms-a trademark, sign, or seal. But an image takes time to develop; it comes
out of experience. Creating a strong consulting image depends on presenting
yourself in a way that reflects your services positively and uniquely. Exhibit 7-7

EXHIBIT 7-7

Elements of a Consultant's Image

Desire
- To be an effective facilitator of organizational change.
- Ability to accept client

Traits
- Empathy toward client situation
- Courage to admit mistakes and use them as learning experiences
- Belief that resolution to client issue will not be perfect
- Motivation to deal with client issue in creative and
- adaptive manner
- Being a sensitive listener
- Willingness to relate to client on an eye-to-eye level

Responsibilities
- Establishing client/consultant relationship characterized by mutual trust and respect.
- Carrying out the consulting assignment in an efficient and punctual manner
- Working through client (or client/consultant) barriers in order to resolve that client issue
- Emphasizing the process toward resolution as well as the resolution itself
- Interacting well by providing feedback and coping with conflicts
- Completing consulting process in an ethical, sincere manner
- Considering effective means (if any) toward continuing
- the consultant/client relationship
- Finding how the consulting assignment can improve the consultant's practice
- Requiring issue resolution to be a joint effort

---

lists some of these characteristics. Your marketing and promotion methods are based on this image. Furthermore, your image will change as you become more aware of ways to satisfy and serve the client.

The essence of your image is interaction-interaction that produces the successful resolution of the client's problems. Your marketing, advertising, and promotion all directly reflect your image. Remember, your image is your call-ing card, a barometer of your personal and professional growth.

SUMMARY AND EXTENSION

As we have demonstrated in a number of ways, advertising and promotion seek to expand contacts and contracts with clients, and enhance and sustain your reputation. There is a large mix of methods and applications to choose from. Being a successful consultant is not based on profit alone; satisfac-tion, innovation, and community service all help to increase your practice's viability. Advertising and promotion can enrich your success, improve your performance, and leave you with greater ethical and cultural sensitivity.

Chapter Eight

Controlling for Profit and Growth

SNAPSHOT

No small business can be successful over the long run without effective procedures to track costs and revenue. In an independent consultancy, all costs are derived basically from two factors: the consultant's labor and the particular contract effort. As we will examine in this chapter, determining a fair rate for your services is the first step in establishing your operating costs.

In addition, your fee is not a mysterious, artificial quantity, but an exact figure computed by specific procedures. This chapter emphasizes using the fee-setting mechanism as a means to ensure proper accounting, fair payment, and proper cost control. In so doing, expenditure losses can be reduced, taxes and other payment addressed precisely, and rates offered that are lower than your competition, thus allowing you a competitive advantage.

SETTING THE FEE

When opening a consulting firm, one of the initial tasks is to determine your fee. A fee does not distinguish between principle and practice, but reflects all costs incurred by the consultant in carrying out an assignment. All fees share common elements, which are illustrated in Exhibit 8-1. The direct labor rate can be determined in a variety of ways. Although you should charge whatever the market will bear, a consultant who wants to build and sustain a solid reputation will usually choose a labor rate that will be maintained regardless of the client's size or sector, and the length and complexity of the project. You might begin by finding out the rates of other professionals-psychiatrists or

---

EXHIBIT 8-1

What Constitutes a Fee?

1. *Direct Labor* (DL). This is the total charge of a consultant's time and professional effort for the assignment. DL is the daily labor rate (DLR) multiplied by the days of consulting effort. The DLR is estimated, based on what other colleagues in your profession or comparable professions charge, your prior job experience, what companies are paying for salaried professionals, or other indicators.

2. *Overhead* (O). This is the total charge of material expenses needed to operate the business prorated for the length of the assignment. O is the daily overhead rate (DOR) multiplied by the days of consulting effort. DOR is computed by estimating the business overhead for a year, then dividing that figure by the number of projected consulting days per year. Once you have estimated the overhead for an assignment, verify that it is in the competitive range by dividing it by the DL.

3. *Administration* (A). This is the total charge of supportive expenses needed to operate the business prorated over the assignment. A is the daily administration rate (DAR) multiplied by the days of consulting effort. DAR is computed by estimating the business administration costs for a year and dividing that figure by projected consulting days. A means for verifying DAR is to divide A by (DL + O).

4. *Profit* (P). This is the return on investment required for taking the risk of operating your consulting business. This money is how your operation remains economically viable. Profit is also a source of financial growth. P is the daily profit rate (DPR) multiplied by the days of consulting effort. DPR is found through historic precedent, competitors' charges, or type of contract relationship. That is, a percentage is chosen and multiplied by (DLR + DOR + DAR).

5. *Direct Expenses* (DE). This is the total charge for all expenses incurred particular to the assignment. A running tab is kept of these expenses and the total amount is added to the factors listed above.

6. *Fee* (F). The fee is the sum of DL, O, A, P, and DE for the length of the assignment. It can be calculated at any point during the consultation.

---

attorneys, for example-in your community, then adjust your rate and multiply this figure by an eight-hour day to obtain your daily labor rate.

In the April 1982 issue of the *Professional Consultant* (published by Howard L. Shenson, Inc., Woodland Hills, CA 91364), a survey of approximately 5100 experienced consultants from various fields revealed for a day's worth of their labor. It is also important to note here that in November 1980, the U.S. government allowed consultants to charge a maximum daily rate of $192. However, for the beginning practitioner, a daily rate of $160 is usually used.

Once you have settled on your daily labor rate, the next step is to calculate your overhead. Exhibit 8-2 lists most, if not all, of the basic expenses to include in your computation. These projections are also helpful for other financial purposes: taxes, business planning, and capital acquisition.

At first, you may not be able to extrapolate all of these operating expenses. In that case, calculate your overhead based on what you know. As you determine other expenses, add them in. The number of consulting days given in Exhibit 8-2 reflects the actual amount of time spent working on client

---

EXHIBIT 8-2

Computing Overhead

Example: Stay well Consulting, Inc.

Overhead Item	Monthly Expense	Yearly Expense
1. Rent and utilities	$ 400	$ 4,800
2. Telephone	120	1,440
3. Photocopying	50	600
4. Stationery and supplies	70	840
5. Clerical assistance	300	3,600
6. Temporary employees	150	1,800
7. Automobile	90	1,080
8. Equipment rental	500	6,000
9. Other*	120	1,440
Total overhead cost	$1,800	$21,600

Now:

Number of consulting days	16	192

Therefore

Daily overhead rate (21,600÷192) is $112.50.

And:
If assume $160 daily labor rate (DLR), then daily overhead rate is 70 percent of DLR.

---

*Includes postage, printing, office lurnishings and maintenance, and miscellaneous

matters. The number is valid whether you work on a fulltime or a part-time basis. The daily overhead rate is computed in the following manner. Assume that there are approximately 21 days per month of work time, then subtract 5 days for sick leave, vacations, and administrative and marketing time, leaving 16 days. Also, items such as clerical assistance and temporary employees are for work done in general support of the business. Specific charges for time spent by these people on individual contracts are noted as a direct expense. For the new consultant, a few tips are in order. Whenever possible, consider sharing equipment and facilities (as mentioned in Chapter Three). This goes for everything from a cooperative office arrangement to sharing part-time employees to joint investment in a long-distance WATS telephone line. There is a certain prestige in having an independent office, yet shared resources also offer you a chance to meet new colleagues, while keeping your overhead costs down. Second, keep accurate records of your overhead expenses. During your first year of operation, you will want to compare your actual costs with your projected costs and make any necessary changes. Also, whenever you add or delete any item from your overhead costs, note the change immediately. Third, a consultant's principle of overhead is liquidity. By keeping costs tied to specific contracts, you can keep down your overhead and overall expenses. Administrative costs are determined in a similar way. Exhibit 8-3 presents the "software" expenses, costs incurred apart from the actual contractual work. New business development, professional enhancement, or extravocational activities constitute this category. Again, based on current data, a percentage relationship exists between direct labor, overhead costs, and administrative costs.

Profit is the next step. Current rates of profit charges to clients run from 8 to 20 percent of the combined total of labor, overhead, and administrative expenses. This rate is computed on a daily basis and multiplied by the days of consulting effort.

Direct expenses, identified in Exhibit 8-4, are incurred for a specific project and computed separately. The subcontracting of any consulting would also constitute a direct expense. Second, per diem rates[1] vary across the United States. (Consult the U.S. Government, *GSA Bulletin,* FPMR-A-40, Supplement 3, 1982, for per diem rates in various cities.)

Third, direct expenses can be billed at any time during the assignment. It is important to maintain good records, but it is often difficult to retain a receipt for every single expense, which is why the miscellaneous entry is important. This category includes items such as postage, courier service, and incidentals (special printing of data tables). The total revenue you request from the

---

[1] A per diem rate is the amount charged the client for your food, lodging, and incidentals on a daily basis while away from home on assignment.

EXHIBIT 8-3

Computing Administration Costs

Administration Item	Monthly Expense	Yearly Expense
1. Business licenses and taxes	$ 40	$ 480
2. Accounting support	60	720
3. Legal support	70	840
4. Employee benefits package*	300	3,600
5. Interest and depreciation	200	2,400
6. Marketing	640	7,680
7. Advertising and promotion	200	2,400
8. Professional activities	100	1,200
Total administration cost	$1,610	$19,320
Now:		
Number of consulting days	16	192

Therefore,

Daily administration rate, DAR
(19,320÷192) is $101

And:

If assume $160 DLR and $112.50 DOR, then from Exhibit 8-1,
DAR = 101 (160 + 112.50) = 37 percent of labor and overhead expense.

---

*Includes health and life insurance, paid vacation, paid sick leave, retirement plan, unemployment compensation, and profit-sharing ... Includes professional association work, dues, educational activities, reading materials, and volunteer efforts.

---

client is based on the sum of your direct labor fee, overhead and administrative costs, profit percentage, and direct expenses. (Note that any accounting technique that you set up for incurred expenses is neither the only one nor the best one. The scheme presented here arranges expenses so that they are easily identified and computed, and comprehensive and applicable to any type of contractual agreement.)

Sample Task I

Critique your fee-setting method by asking yourself the following questions: What factors do I use to set my fee? Do the elements for each cost factor vary from contract to contract? How do I combine all of these cost factors? Is using the KISS (Keep It Simple and Stated) method a better way of tracking costs?

EXHIBIT 8-4

Estimate of Direct Expenses

Example: ILLSAIL Shipping Company
Consulting February 3-March 6, 1983

Direct Expenses	*Explanation*	*Amount*
1. Computer time and materials	10 days @ $40	$ 400
2. Clerical	12 days @ $40	480
3. Reproduction	8 days @ $100	800
4. Telephone	1 month	100
5. Transportation Air travel		
Auto travel	3 trips @ $110 +	650
6. Per diem	4 trips @ $80 90 miles @ 20<t/mile	18
7. Miscellaneous	12 days @ $80	960
Total		260
		$3,668

Let's assume that you are bidding on a contract to design an automated inventory system for boat parts. Your daily labor rate is $160.00, daily overhead rate is $112.50, daily administrative rate is $101.00, and your profit is 15 percent of the total of these three figures. Exhibit 8-5 demonstrates how you use the percentage method to reach a cost estimate. Having usable

---

EXHIBIT 8-5

Cost Proposal for Automating a Shipbuilder's Inventory

Item	*Amount*
1. Direct labor Senior Consultant: 20 days @ $160	$ 3,200
2. Overhead (70% of item 1)	2,240
3. Subtotal (items 1 + 2)	5,440
4. Administration (37% of item 3)	2,013
5. Subtotal (items 3 + 4)	7,453
6. Profit (15% of item 5)	1,118
7. Direct expenses (see Exhibit 8-4)	3,668
8. Total: Fee (items 5 + 6 + 7)	$12,239

EXHIBIT 8-6

Alternative Method of Cost Estimating:

The Composite Day Quote

Item	Daily Amount
1. Direct labor	$ 160.00
2. Overhead (70% of item 1)	112.00
3. Administration (37% of items 1 + 2)	101.00
4. Profit (15% of item 1 − item 3)	56.00
5. Items 1 + 2 + 3 + 4 = the composite day quote (CDQ)	428.54
6. Contract term: 20 days (CDQ × 20)	8,570.80
7. Direct expenses	3,668.00
8. Total proposed costs (fee)	$12,238.80

---

estimates for direct labor, overhead, and administrative costs allows you to bid quickly on proposals. Changes in your rates can be easily incorporated, guaranteeing an accurate and competitive bidding position.

There is an alternative means of providing cost estimates. Often, a client will ask the prospective consultant for his or her daily rate, charges per day, or price quote. All of these terms mean the same thing. What the consultant does is compute his or her operating and labor expenses plus profit for, in this case, an eight-hour day. Exhibit 8-6 shows how this is done for the shipbuilding contract discussed in Exhibit 8-5. All business costs are computed for the life of the assignment-20 days. Direct expenses are added to this figure, giving the total amount needed to complete the project. Both estimating methods are identical and should be used together to double check your computations, as well as for effective marketing.

Sample Task II

Given the following specifications: total cost, $24,998; direct expenses, $5,200.

1. Find the composite day quote for 2 weeks, 5 weeks, and 10 weeks of direct labor.
2. Using Exhibit 8-5, compute the direct labor, overhead, administration, and profit for a five-week project.
3. What improvements can you make to the overhead and administration rate?
4. What effect(s) would these improvements have on profit and direct labor charge?

As shown in Exhibit 5-6, there are four major ways to contract for services: fixed price, time and material, cost plus fee, and retainer. How is the cost proposal illustrated in Exhibit 8-5 modified to accommodate these different contracting methods? Let's examine each type of contract.

Fixed Price. In most situations, the consultant's cost estimate must first be accepted by the client (usually following a negotiation). The client then agrees to pay the consultant the amount stated, no more and no less, for completing the prescribed assignment. If the consultant finishes the work at less cost than the stated budget, the savings is his or her additional profit.

Conversely, if the consultant completes the assignment over budget the additional expenses incurred are paid by the consultant. There are two modifications to Exhibit 8-5 that are worth noting. First, where there is an extended time frame for the assignment, a cost-of-living adjustment clause is added to increase the daily rate for labor, overhead, or administration.

Second, a client might add a performance fee as an inducement for, say, earlier delivery of results or longer monitoring of the implemented procedures.

Time and material. This arrangement is identical to the fixed-price contract except for one important element-there is no set time frame. That is, the consultant bills the client for work done at agreed-to rates for as long as it takes to accomplish the assignment. Generally, the consultant determines the minimum and maximum number of days to do the job, and the client agrees to pay the costs incurred in that time period only.

Cost plus fee. Here the client agrees to pay the consultant's estimate plus any additional costs incurred up to a predetermined level. This level could be a percentage of the total cost estimate, a percentage of the total cost element, or a fixed amount. Generally, the consultant does not have a cost overrun, but care must be taken in defining which costs the client will pay. For example, if the consultant is to be paid a daily labor rate for the length of the project, as estimated in the proposal, and the client agrees to pay for all of the consultant's direct expenses over the life of the contract, then the consultant will not be reimbursed for additional days.

Retainer. This is essentially a part-ti me, fixed-price contract. The consultant contracts to provide services for a set number of days a month. The agreement is open-ended, but the amount of consulting given each billing period is set.

Many clients perceive fee setting and contracting as a magical trick. It is important to let the client know how you arrive at your daily labor rate and composite day quote, to discuss which kind of contractual relationship is most suitable, and to stick with the arrangement.

Before leaving this subject, a related point should be aired. When you change your fees, it is wise to do it in two stages. For your new clients, set a rate as of a specified date. However, let a few months pass before you increase rates to old clients. To avoid problems at billing time, let your clients know beforehand whenever you are setting new rates. If your profit or company status changes do not hesitate to inform clients. Remember, regular communication with clients can open up future consulting opportunities.

Case Example 8-1: The Free Exchange

A few years ago I was called in by a birdseed manufacturing company to correct the ineffective use of secretarial services. I was given the following information: the pool of secretaries was large, often idle, and unproductive when busy; improvements in the work environment had no effect on the secretaries' motivation, and as a result management was farming out clerical tasks to outside temporary service agencies.

At my first meeting with the client we agreed that the root causes of secretarial dissatisfaction were not known. We also agreed that short-term, intermediate, and long-term solutions were in order. I said that I would get to work as soon as I completed my current assignments. The client was enthusiastic- that is, until we began discussing contract arrangements.

She thought that an equitable arrangement was an agreed-to sum covering all labor, indirect, and direct costs. "You mean a fixed-price contract?" I asked. "Yes," she replied, "fixed price is fine as far as it goes." "But in this case," I answered, "the issue and its resolution are not well defined. Your situation is more amenable to a cost-plus-variable fee arrangement. That is, the estimate I submit to you will cover all of my consulting. If the estimate is exceeded, you will pay for all the costs up to seven months following the implementation of the short-term resolution. If more work is required after seven months, we will formulate a part-time retainer. How does that sound to you?"

"It sounds," she replied angrily, "like I am being taken for a ride. What do you mean the issue is not well defined? Do you think that we are made of money? There is no way that I will agree to write a blank check for you!"

"Hold on," I said calmly, "I am not requesting a free hand in the till. What I am trying to explain is that your situation is not clearly understood by anyone. Your secretaries are not motivated, and your overhead is suffering. I propose solving these problems, but I need your cooperation. Alleviating employee dissatisfaction does not happen overnight, nor does management suddenly regain confidence in its clerical staff.

All of these changes take time, and this translates into charges for my services. Look, you didn't pick my name out of the *Yellow Pages;* I came to you well-referenced and experienced. I propose the following: I will submit a proposal outlining my approach to solving the problems, the projected expenses, and a method of payment. We will review each phase before I begin to ensure that it is the proper next step, an equitable expense, and can produce the desired results. This way the only deficit that will occur is the shortage of apathy, unnecessary expense, and high overhead by secretaries and managers alike. Shall I go ahead with my proposal?"

ASSURING PAYMENT

No matter what type of contract you use, the consulting arrangement is binding because each party has agreed to give the other a tangible service.

The consultant receives money for helping the client resolve an issue. Unfortunately, in far too many instances receiving payment from clients becomes an issue in itself.

As shown in Chapter Five, the consulting contract can specify the type, frequency, and at times, default conditions for payment. In most situations, the consultant submits an itemized invoice detailing all expenditures for a stated time period. An example is given in Exhibit 8-7. Such invoices are usually sent to the client at agreed-upon intervals.

As mentioned in Chapter Five, if the client fails to reimburse the consultant in a timely fashion, interest may be charged. If several invoices go unpaid, the consultant can terminate his or her services (as shown in Exhibit 5-8). Before additional steps are taken to secure funds, notify the client of the delinquent payments. If the client does not respond to these communications, the consultant can either turn the matter over to a collection agency or bring suit against the client. It has been my experience that both methods are time consuming and expensive, but your lawyer is apt to give you due process sooner than a collection agency. However, in some cases, this situation can be avoided by checking the client's financial solvency before you do any work. You can ask a credit bureau for the client's credit rating, obtain a copy of the annual report, talk with other consultants who have dealt with the firm, or use other methods.

KEEPING ACCURATE RECORDS

As discussed in Chapter Two, finding a competent and compatible CPA is a way to stay solvent and successful, but a CPA's performance depends on your efforts. Accurate and easy-to-use ledgers and forms assure a minimum of

EXHIBIT 8-7

Sample Invoice

Date

Consultant Letterhead

Client Address

Dear

I submit this invoice for professional services rendered to your firm,

_____ from August 15, 1982, to October 1, 1982. The itemized expenses incurred are with regard to Contract ACD/3, "Feasibility of Hydronic Sprinkler Systems." As stated in the contract, terms are payment due upon receipt. For any questions, please contact A. Rank at (301)662-8884.

Professional Services	*Date*	*Amount*
1. Literature review	8/17–8/25	$ 900
2. Meeting with J. Paul	8/27	75
3. Literature synopsis and	9/1–9/4	330
annotation	9/16	125
4. Presentation of research	8/15–10/1	$1,430
Total services (includes direct labor, overhead, and administration charges, plus profit)		

Direct Expenses (Receipts Attached)	*Date*	*Amount*
1. Auto costs	8/17–9/16	$ 110
2. Photocopying	8/17–9/16	203
3. Clerical and report production	8/17–9/16	157
Total direct expenses	8/15–10/1	470
Total amount payable	10/1	$1,900

Authorized Signature *A. Rank*

financial entanglements with your clients, the Internal Revenue Service, and your accountant. Some accounting forms worth having are:

Calendar of activities. Obtain a pocket calendar to record the following daily items:

1. Number of hours worked logged in by contract number or administrative function
2. Overhead or administrative costs incurred
3. Direct expenses noted by contract number
4. Comments for accounting/things to do

At the end of each week, record a summary of hours, costs, and revenues (see Exhibit 8-8). The summary and the daily entries can be brief, backed up

---

EXHIBIT 8-8

Weekly Activity Summary (Example)

Week Ending 1/9/83

		Activity		
	Direct Labor	*Direct Labor*	*Material*	
Factor	*Hours*	*Cost*	*Cost*	*Total*
Overhead*			$450	$450
Rent and utilities			—	
Telephone			—	—
Photocopying			50	50
Stationery and supplies			100	100
Clerical assistance			225	225
Temporary employees			—	—
Automobile			—	—
Equipment rental			—	—
Other (postage)			75	75

Administration*	6	$120	120	240
Business license and taxes	—	—	20	20
Accounting support	1	20	—	20
Legal support	1	20	—	20
Employee benefits package	—	—	—	—
Interest and depreciation	—	—	—	—
Marketing	2	40	—	40
Advertising and promotion	1	20	30	50
Professional activities	1	20	70	90

Contract Number

Factor	A1	A2	A3	Total
Direct labor hours	12	18	—	30
Direct labor cost	$240	$360	—	$600
Direct expense*	$285	50	$215	550
Computer time and materials	100	—	120	220
Clerical	20	40	20	80
Reproduction	—	—	45	45
Telephone	15	10	30	55
Transportation	110	—	—	110
Air travel	90	—	—	90
Auto travel	20	—	—	20
Other	~			
Per diem	—	—	40	40
Miscellaneous	—	—		—
Revenue	Amount			

Received	$2000
Billed	700
Owed this week	600
Past due	3100
Revenue outstanding	3700
Totals	Amount
Direct labor	$ 600
Overhead	450
Administration	240
Direct expenses	550
Composite costs	1840
Revenue	2000
Net profit	160

* Expense documentation recorded.

with invoices or receipts as needed. It is crucial in beginning a new business to record and analyze your efforts, so that effective corrections and improvements can be made.

Contract budget sheet. To keep tabs on the revenue requirements for a particular contract, Exhibit 8-9 is used. The monthly project costs, revenue received, and net income are all stated. A net income of zero or more supports a positive cash flow. A negative net income must be watched carefully.

Overhead and administration control sheets. Over the life of the contract, overhead and administration controls are kept for all firm activities (see Exhibits 8-10 and 8-11). Running tabulations for these cost items are kept for the entire year. These sheets are used to verify and update overhead and administration percentage rates, and also act as the indirect cost ledgers for the cash disbursements journal, which is used for calculating taxes.

***Direct** expense sheets.* Since direct expenses are a function of a particular contract, two sheets are used. One, Exhibit 8-12, shows the direct expenses incurred for various contracts on a monthly basis. This sheet is used to keep track of all direct expenses and to assess ways to reduce

EXHIBIT 8-9

Contract Budget Sheet

Contract Title ______		Contract No ______			
Client Name ______		Client Agency ______			
Contract Duration ______					
	Time Period				
Cost Factor	*May*	*June*	*July*	*Aug*	*Sept.*
Direct labor (DL)					
Overhead (O) (70% of DL)					
Administration item(A) (37% of DL + O)					
Profit (15% of DL + O + A)					
Subtotal					
Direct expenses					
Total costs					
Total revenue received					
Total revenue outstanding					

such costs. The other direct expense sheet, Exhibit 8-13, is the direct cost ledger comprising the cash disbursement journal used for calculating taxes.

Finally, Exhibit 8-8 is a sample form used to record all weekly direct expenses. These weekly sheets make up the monthly summary, Exhibit 8-14.

Direct labor sheet. Keep track of your hours in a pocket calendar or notebook. Then enter the hours on a weekly time sheet like Exhibit 8-15.

This information can then be converted into dollars by dividing the hours by an eight-hour day and multiplying by your direct labor rate. These figures can then be fed into Exhibit 8-16.

The information system created in Exhibits 8-10 through 8-16 can now be used to compute taxes, plan for profit, and control costs.

EXHIBIT 8-10

Overhead Control Sheet

	Month			
Overhead Item	*May*	*June*	*July*	*Aug.*
Rent and utilities				
Telephone				
Photocopying				
Stationery and supplies				
Clerical assistance				
Temporary employees				
Automobile				
Equipment rental				
Other				
Total				

EXHIBIT 8-11

Administration Control Sheet

	Month			
Administration Item	*May*	*June*	*July*	*Aug.*
Business license and taxes				
Accounting support				
Legal support				
Employee benefits package				
Administration Item May June				
Interest and depreciation				
Marketing				
Advertising and promotion				
Professional activities				
Total				

EXHIBIT 8-12

Direct Expense control Sheet

Month _____

Contract

Expense Item	A1	A2	A3	A4	Total
Computer time and materials					
Clerical					
Reproduction					
Telephone					
Transportation					
Air travel					
Auto travel					
Other					
Per diem					
———days@$80					
Miscellaneous					
Total					

EXHIBIT 8-13

Expense Statement

Contract Title _____   Contract No _____
Purpose of Trip _____

Expense Item	Date	Total
Air travel		
_____		
_____		
_____		
Auto travel		
miles @ C/mile		
Parking and tolls		

Taxi and bus fares Meals*		
Lodging*		
"Telephone*		
Reproduction*		
Clerical*		
Computer time and materials*		
Other (explain)		
Daily total		
Grand total		
Cash advance		
Balance due		
"Attach receipts		

Submitted by: _____

Date: _____

EXHIBIT 8-14

Direct Expense Summary

	Month				
Expense Item	*May*	*June*	*July*	*Aug*	*Sept*
Computer time and materials					
Clerical					
Reproduction					
Telephone					
Transportation					
Per diem					
Miscellaneous					
Total					

EXHIBIT 8-15

Direct Labor Time Sheet

Time Period	Contract				Weekly Totals
	A1	A2	A3	A4	
Week of 5/6					
Week of 5/13					
Week of 5/27					
Total May					
Week of 6/3					
Week of 6/10					
Week of 6/17					
Week of 6/24					
Total June					

EXHIBIT 8-16

Monthly Cash Flow Status

	Time Period				
Factor	May	June	July	Aug.	Sept
Direct labor					
Overhead*					
Overhead match (%)					
Administration†					
Administration match (%)					
Direct expense					
Contract A1					
Contract A2					
Contract A3					
Contract A4					
Total costs					

Revenue					
Contract A1					
Contract A2					
Contract A3					
Contract A4					
Other					
Revenue outstanding					
Profit‡					
Profit match					

*Overhead is assumed 70 percent of direct labor,

† Administration is assumed 37 percent of direct labor and overhead,

‡ Profit is assumed 15 percent of direct labor, overhead, and administration.

Sample Task III

Start with Exhibit 8-16. Work with two contracts. Pick arbitrary time totals for two months. Assume that your direct labor rate (per day) is $200. Using the percentage given in Exhibit 8-6, find the cost for labor, overhead, administration, and profit for each contract for each month. Now, assume that the total revenue for the first contract is $16,000 per month and $20,000 for the second. What is the largest direct expense figure that you could incur such that your net income would be 20 percent for each contract?

PAYING YOUR TAXES

Taxes have become a collective American evil; no one likes to pay them.

However, the professional consultant must pay federal, state, and local taxes. To avoid paying unnecessary or excess taxes, you should maintain accurate records.

A competent accountant is an asset to any consultant, but you also must be knowledgeable about taxes-when they are due and why, what is taxable and what is not. And you must be prepared to change your bookkeeping.

First, arrange a meeting with your accountant. Remember that you are the client in this case, so follow your own recommendations for choosing a consultant (see Exhibit 8-17). Next, decide on a fee, the information you need to supply, and when and how your financial planning will be done.

EXHIBIT 8-17

Using Accounting Services

Why

Lack experience preparing taxes

Certification in case of legal actions

Helps keep you out of legal difficulties

Assist in taking all deductions possible

Who

Through personal or professional referral

Through association recommendations Is fee competitive?

Can I establish a working relationship with this person?

How

Meet to establish accounting controls

Plan tax payments and deductions

Seek assistance in long-term financial planning

Ask advice on particular accounting problems

When

Meet before tax year is over to plan

Meet after tax year to review taxes and financial controls

Planning requires data compiled from accurate records. When paying taxes, five types of records are kept, as described in Exhibit 8-18. A cash receipts journal is kept to record all income received. A sample sheet from such a journal is illustrated in Exhibit 8-9. All invoices or payment slips are kept as well. The data from these slips are entered in this exhibit and in Exhibit 8-8 for monthly time periods. Similarly, data from checks or credit slips are entered into Exhibits 8-10 through 8-12, making up the cash disbursements journal. In addition, any small expenses incurred are entered into the petty cash ledger. The ledgers and the accompanying sale slips, receipts, and invoices are used to determine your taxes and should be kept for up to seven years, in case of an IRS audit.

Further, as an unincorporated proprietorship or partnership, you must pay self-employment tax, which covers social security benefits and is not

---

EXHIBIT 8-18

Inputs for Income Taxes

Cash *Receipts Journal*
    Income from contract work
    Interest income
    Other income

Cash Disbursements Journal
    Overhead expense sheets
    Administration expense sheets
    Direct expense sheet summaries

Petty Cash Fund
    Voucher slip sheets

---

a deductible business expense. Thus, if your combined self-employment and income taxes are greater than $100, you are required to prepay them in quarterly installments. You must pay estimated taxes on April 15, June 15, September 15, and January 15 of the taxable year. If at least 80 percent of your taxes are not prepaid, you are subject to IRS penalties and interest. For the beginning consultant, this payment schedule could hurt more than help business; yet proper write-offs can offset the tax burden. Finally, effective filing of your taxes can be an effective way to estimate the profitability of your business.

If your firm is incorporated, you are an "employee" of the corporation and thus draw a salary. Your personal income and social security taxes will be withheld and remitted on a periodic basis as part of the payroll system.

CARRYING OUT FORECASTING AND CONTROL

Consultants are by nature planners. Whenever a consultant quotes a price for services, he or she is predicting how much time will be required by the client. However, self-forecasting is another matter because many consultants do not have the skill to sit down and project their own activities. After marketing, this projection is the most important activity. Why? Because as shown in Chapter Three, a firm's goals are realized by making and carrying out forecasts.

Since this book is designed to be pragmatic and useful, no time will be wasted on forecasting models. Instead, we will show you how to do a forecast, and how to evaluate its results. First, assume that ARCO is in its second year of operation as a management consulting firm. In the first week of February a quarterly projection is made of activity for March through June. Prior forecasts have used a profit and loss statement format to project profit potential. Now, using Exhibit 4-14-the current marketing status report and the last projected profit and loss statement-Exhibit 8-19 is produced. Let's run through the viewgraph carefully. Revenue includes three elements: leads (the expected services the consultant hopes to procure), prospects (the services procured but not yet performed), and contracts (the ongoing consulting assignments). In the proposals and letters of agreement or contracts for all these services, a figure has been given for the monthly costs of the professional labor. The overhead and administrative expenses are projected as percentages of the direct labor (specifically using these percentages of Exhibit 8-5). Direct expenses are aggregated from an itemized breakdown that is not shown.

Now, the gross profit is the percent of profit desired (in this case the figures come from Exhibit 8-15). Taxes are computed as the sum of self-employment plus income (as mentioned above), and the net income to this sole proprietorship is stated last.

Now the same dollar amounts are computed for the actual expenditures in the middle of June. Exhibit 8-20 shows the projected figures alongside the real ones. The actual revenue amounts were taken from the entries in the cash receipts journal. The direct labor and expenses were calculated from Exhibits 8-10 through 8-15. The gross profit equals the revenues minus the labor and expense costs. This amount (15.4 percent) is in the desired range of 15 percent used to calculate the composite day quote (see Exhibit 8-6). The actual situation displays additional unexpected income from existing contracts to balance the lack of hoped-for revenue from leads. The total revenue was $2,500, less than the projected figure. Yet the gross profit averaged higher (as a percentage of labor, overhead, and administration costs) than the projected quantity. This is due to two factors: the March direct labor costs were lower than expected, and the direct expenses were down across the three-month period. Even though administration costs rose in April and May (to 45 percent of labor and overhead), overhead costs were as expected and thus did not decrease the hoped-for profit. Finally, this consultant's good bookkeeping system enabled his accountant to predict accurately the amount of tax due.

Before leaving this topic, there is an additional facet of accounting cost control-to explore. Its three facets are: profit margin, waste reduction, and

EXHIBIT 8-19

Income Forecast, ARCO, INC

Projected Item	March	April	May	March	April	May	Actual Comments
Revenue	$8,000	$6,000	$10,000				
Leads	2,000	—	4,000				
Prospects	1,000	1,000	2,000				
Contracts	5,000	5,000	4,000				
Direct Labor	2,560	1,920	3,200				@$160/day
Operating expense							
Overhead	1,792	1,344	2,240				70% of DL
Administration	1,610	1,208	2,013				37% of DL+O
Direct expense	1,200	900	1,500				
Total expense	$7,162	$5,372	$8,953				
Gross profit	$838	$628	$8,953				@14% of (DL+O+A)
total profit (March-May)	$2,513						
Taxes (39% bracket)	$1,000						
Net profit (March-May)							

EXHIBIT 8-20

Income Forecast, Arco, Inc.

Projected Item	March	April	May	March	April	May	Actual Comments
Revenue	$8,000	$6,000	$10,000	$6,000	$7,000	$8,500	
Leads				-0-	-0-	-0-	No accrued revenue
Prospects				1,000	-0-	1,500	
Contracts				5,000	7,000	7,000	Extension of two contracts
Direct Labor	2,560	1,920	3,200	1,760	2,240	2,720	
Operating expense							
Overhead				1,232	1,568	1,904	Decrease in telephone; purchase of photocopier
Administration				1,107	1,714	2,081	Borrowed money
Direct expense				900	800	850	Decrease in planned travel
Total expense	7,162	5,372	8,953	4,999	6,322	7,555	
Gross profit				1,001	678	945	Average percent of labor overhead, and administration is 15.4
total profit (March-May)		2,513			2,624		
Taxes (39% bracket)					1,114		
Net profit (March-May)		$1,513			$1,510		Coincidence

growth potential. The profit margin is a function of how large you wish your profit to be. Realistically, this is relative to competing firms. The January 1982 economic survey of the consulting profession produced 5,100 responses (as discussed above). Two areas are of interest here. The respondents charged 9 percent of every expense dollar to profit and 28 percent of each expense dollar for direct labor. In our example, the profit margin and direct labor are greater than the industry average. Our percentages imply that while profits are being made, the potential for continued profits could be enhanced if costs are kept down. Further, the projection of Exhibit 8-19 showed the consultant working at a maximum number of 21 consulting days per month (as discussed above). But the actual labor figures indicated a three-day availability per month for more consulting. This time could be used seeking new clients or enhancing the practice through educational, advertising, or promotion activities. Profit planning has another side as well: reducing waste. Waste comes in many forms; Exhibit 8-21 points out a few of the key areas. A program for improving your consulting practice's efficiency is outlined here:

- Recognize that the waste is occurring.
- Identify primary areas of inefficiency.
- Rank problems.
- Develop means of reducing waste for each problem area in turn.
- Implement and monitor solutions.
- Fine-tune all areas affected.
- Maintain and improve efficiency techniques.

Waste is both a quantitative and a qualitative factor in consulting.

Correcting these abuses requires a concerted effort. But do not let it dismay you; there is plenty of available help, and whatever program and skills you develop to find and eliminate waste} make sure that you document them for future use.

Before we leave this topic, there is one more subject worth discussing: how to increase your revenue without increasing your fee. Particularly when you are getting started or are experiencing a slow time} you can try to:

- Set a minimum number of days for any contract.
- Charge for full days.
- Make use of client facilities and equipment.
- Negotiate a performance bonus.
- Obtain an advance for direct expenses.

The return from these pointers can sustain your solvency.

EXHIBIT 8-21

Waste in the Consulting Practice

Outside Services Ignored
- Does own accounting
- Does own legal counseling
- Does not belong to professional associations
- Does not seek learning opportunities
- Does not ask for advice from colleagues about practice

Lack of Office Management
- Keeps incomplete or unorganized records
- Uses telephone, photocopier, office at high rates when less costly alternatives are available
- Spends most of administration time running errands and has little time to plan for expansion
- Does not have presentable office space for receiving clients
- Fails to keep calendar of activities

Shortcomings in Consulting Engagements
- Keeps sporadic contact with client
- Has no plan and budget of how contract will operate
- Lacks a marketing approach
- Does not follow up communication with past clients
- Spends little if any time in honest reflection about client concerns and issues

---

Sample Task IV

Refer to Exhibit 8-21 and ask yourself the following question: If I were to assess how my telephone expenses could be reduced} I would try the following:

1. See where most of the expense is: day calls, toll calls} long-distance calls} and so on.
2. Reduce expenses through:
   a. Decreasing number of outgoing calls.
   b. Calling in off-peak hours.
   c. Asking clients to call me back} whenever possible.
   d. Purchase cheaper local or long-distance service.
   e. Pool telephone use with other professionals.

Now pick one of the other areas mentioned and follow the suggested steps to improve efficiency. What are your findings? How soon can you enact the changes?

Your firm's growth potential is covered in more detail in Chapter Twelve. For now, it is sufficient to point out the major avenues open to you:

• Diversify markets.
• Expand range of services.
• Enter into more subcontract work or joint ventures.
• Increase daily rate.
• Enlarge size of staff.

These avenues are a function of marketing success and your desire to form a consulting organization. However, such success will be short-lived if contracts are poorly managed, clients are ineffectively treated, and no effort is taken to develop your professional standing. It is not only a question of being well organized; it is knowing how much consulting activity you can handle and handle well. Therefore, the first step in achieving growth is to continue the business long enough to expand. If it turns out that you are short of working capital for a few months, a short term loan could provide the needed cushion. As described in Chapter Two, having an accurate picture of your operations and a well-defined purpose for the borrowed funds at the time of a loan request (such as Exhibits 8-8 and 8-19) can help you meet the criteria for approval. Having outstanding loans is not a negative factor. In fact, in most cases, loans are needed to cover operating expenses until contract payments are received. The interest from the loan can be offset by securing new business.

Sample Task V

In growing consulting firms, there is an unavoidable practice of charging expenses to one contract that were incurred by working on another contract. This phenomenon occurs because of the time lag of payment for consulting efforts. Devise a method to keep track of expenses which does not ((rob Peter to pay Paulo" How would you avoid cost overruns using this scheme?

SUMMARY AND EXTENSION

The information given in these pages reflects a desire to identify and use efficient cost-control techniques. The procedures take time to set up and discipline to maintain. You must also be willing to modify them as your business grows. However, the results are well worth it. One topic that has not been addressed is varying fees for different clients. Generally, your reputation is based on fairness, quality, and completeness. As discussed, your fee can change over time as costs increase, your reputation grows, or the nature of your services varies. However, charging different fees to clients is frowned upon even though there might be a time when a client will request a special rate for your services. Or you might alter your fee schedule to entice a new client or collect on a delinquent account. Yet once you open the door to this practice, it stays open-with subsequent loss of revenue. As shown in Chapter Five, the way not to give away business is to state clearly the services that you are providing. If the client cannot afford your fee, provide a level of service that he or she can pay for. As shown in the next chapter, consistency in fee setting makes economic and ethical sense.

Chapter Nine

Practicing Ethics in Everyday Consulting

SNAPSHOT

As we indicated in Chapter One, consultants come from an array of professions, backgrounds, and experiences. Even though most consultants have been exposed to ethical concepts, few spend time focusing on ethical concerns. In this chapter we present an ethical code and its application to current consulting practices. The ethics of gaining an "inside track" with the federal government and the question of professional liability are two of the issues raised here. The objective of this chapter is to involve the client in your use of ethics and to involve your peers in the discussion and use of ethical practices.

ESTABLISHING AN ETHICAL CODE

The work performed by consultants includes the transaction of services, feelings, and values. Defining ethics, morals, and ethical code and values is an appropriate place to begin our discussion. A dictionary definition of ethics is that they are principles of conduct governing an individual or a profession. It is assumed that consultants act as professionals: that is, as persons practicing common concepts and skills which have collectively gained them a reputation. These principles of conduct (ethics) are derived from considerations of what is right and what is wrong-morals. Morals help define accepted patterns of social and personal relations. Together, these principles and morals are used to form standards of behavior, that is, an ethical code. How closely people adhere to these principles (that is, how ethical they are) determines the degree to which enforcement measures and supplemental education are required.

In terms of consulting, ethics can sustain an individual's success, ensure equitable and satisfactory client relationships, and stimulate the consultant's desire to make a meaningful contribution to society. In most professions, an ethical code exists to protect the client's interests, to state principles of professional conduct in writing, and to motivate the practitioner to use such principles beyond the requirements of law. Many consulting associations have established ethical codes (for example, the Association of Consulting Management Engineers; the American Society for Training and Development; the Academy of Management, Divisions on Organization Development and Managerial Consultation; the Independent Computer Consultants Association; the Operations Research Society of America; and the Institute of Management Consultants). Exhibit 9-1 displays standards of behavior defined by the Association of Consulting Management Engineers and the Institute of Management Consultants.

Sample Task I

Critique Exhibit 9-1 using the following criteria:

- How often does each standard apply to my consulting practice?
- How important is each ethical principle to my behavior?
- How deficient is the precept in normal client/consultant relationships?
- What is the difficulty in consulting assignments in incorporating the standard described?

Next, answer these questions:

1. How could an ethical code deal with a negative situation in a consulting assignment?
2. What are the tangible and intangible effects of following an ethical code? What impact does this code have on a consultant's reputation?
3. Conversely, how could a consultant's reputation sometimes give false credibility?
4. State three ways to transmit an ethical code to the clients. Which one(s) do you prefer, and why?

Sample Task II

List five ethical concerns you or your colleagues have dealt with. (If you are new to consulting, list five ethical concerns you have as a professional.)

EXHIBIT 9-1

Consulting Code of Ethics

Responsibilities to the Client. The Consultant:
1. Places Client interests ahead of Consultant interests, and serves such interests with integrity, competence, and independence.
2. Maintains confidentiality in the course of the assignment. This precept holds true for assignment results until released by the Client.
3. Informs Client of factors that might impair judgment or objectivity and provides contingencies to handle them.
4. Performs each Client engagement to meet the defined needs of the Client, and develops recommendations which can be implemented promptly and efficiently.
5. Charges fees commensurate with the nature of the services performed and the responsibility assumed.
6. Integrates professional accomplishments and changes into the consulting process, and keeps the Client informed of these.
7. Makes no offer of employment to employees of Client without prior Client consent.
8. Presents results or advice in an objective, complete, and honest manner.
9. Notes the full contribution made by the Client to the consulting engagement.

Responsibilities to the Potential Client. The Consultant:
1. Offers no inducement other than experience, ability, and reputation.
2. Presents qualifications in a truthful and dignified manner.
3. Accepts only those engagements where qualified to undertake them, and which will provide benefits to the Client.
4. Submits a proposal of work to be performed and its cost before the assignment begins.
5. Charges no fees contingent on any specific result.

Responsibilities to Other Consultants or Clients. The Consultant:
1. Serves two or more competing Clients only with their mutual consent.
2. Accepts an engagement with a Client while another consulting firm is serving the Client only if there will be no conflict of interest in doing so.
3. Refuses to displace another Consultant if a Client has made a proper, legal commitment to that Consultant.
4. Reviews the work of another Consultant for the same Client only with the knowledge of such Consultant.

5. Refuses to accept fees or pay fees to others for Client referrals.
6. Recruits Consultants from other consulting firms only with prior firm approval.
7. Reports unethical conduct of Consultants to professional associations, and, if need be, to other authorities.

Responsibilities to Self. The Consultant:
1. Gains and upgrades the knowledge, skills, and practices of consulting.
2. Joins one or more professional associations, and upholds the ethical principles of them.
3. Carries out each engagement through the direction of a qualified project director. Competent support persons will provide effective services throughout the consulting process as needed.
4. Reserves the right to withdraw from the assignment if his or her conduct is sorely impaired.
5. Refuses to accept fees or other inducements from individuals or organizations whose equipment, supplies, or services might be used during the Client engagement.
6. Advertises services in a nonderogatory fashion.

Responsibilities to the Public. The Consultant:
1. Keeps the public informed of consulting advances.
2. Contributes to the understanding of better ways to manage the institutions of our society.
3. Inspires confidence, respect, and trust through open communication and regard for mores and expectations of the community in which the consulting activity takes place.

Describe how you handled or would handle each ethical concern. What changes took place in the consulting process and at which steps?

An ethical code is meaningful only if it is incorporated into professional activities. Simply establishing a code of behavior does not guarantee changes in the way in which consultants function. Therefore, there is a need for devising a way to use and enforce the code.

In addition, an ethical code must change as the profession evolves. For example, today, consultants are concerned with the following issues:

• Serving on *the board of the client company*. Can a consultant still be objective and loyal to the client if he or she sits on the board?

- *Combining consulting with executive recruiting.* Should the management consultant who recommends sacking the president of the client organization be given the assignment to fill that slot? Can the consultant fulfill his or her responsibilities to the client?
- *Becoming* a *whistle blower.* Should a consultant report crimes committed by the client when it is in the public interest to do so?
- *Allowing the consultant* name *to be used for endorsement* of *the client or client products.* Does this action jeopardize the consultant's reputation?

Different ethical concerns are manifested at different stages of the consulting process. In the selection stage, the client tends to implicitly (if not explicitly) seek out a consultant who shares his or her values. However, each party should inform the other of his or her values and be ready to accept the consequences of such action, including the consultant's refusal to work for a client.

In addition, confidentiality concerns need to be aired and addressed.

During the search for solutions to the client's problem, the consultant should not exaggerate the desirability of implementing the suggested changes and ignore the importance of potential barriers to enacting these changes. Finally, when consultants are instituting changes in the client organization, they must note the degree of control being exerted over the client's behavior. One way to deal with this dilemma is to have the client institute the changes incrementally. Seven hundred and ninety-one respondents to a questionnaire sent to five professional associations indicated that the consultant is obliged to discuss any conflict that arises.

A consultant's objectivity does not necessitate a value-free relationship with the client; consultants do have opinions, attitudes, and feelings and can use them to their advantage. That is, the consultant can try to incorporate varied ethical precepts in his or her practice to make it value full.

Such actions can enhance communication and assist the consultant in reaching a mutual accommodation between the client's expectations and the consultant's.

SPECIAL TOPIC: PAYING THE PRICE FOR
THE INSIDE TRACK?

In trying to secure new contracts, consulting firms are tempted like any other type of business. Often, gaining sales requires marketing people to resort to tactics that give the firm that extra competitive edge or, in some cases, noncompetitive advantage. A series of articles in the *Washington Post* (June 22–26, 1980) described the lack of competition, system inadequacies, personal influences, and other abuses in the federal government's procurement offices. Many of these weaknesses have existed for a long time, yet we will examine the fundamental ethics in marketing consulting services, focusing on marketing methods, results, and the consequences for the profession.

Marketing methods. "Many in the contracting business say that the real competition for contracts is to be found here, in the marketing arena. It is competition to develop an inside track" *(Washington Post,* June 26, 1980). An inside track is commonly defined as a position of advantage in competition. The key word here is "advantage," for if the advantage is fair, it can enhance and sustain the competitive procedures; if the advantage is unfair, it can thwart and belittle the contracting procedures. Exhibit 9-2 displays examples of gaining a fair or unfair competitive advantage in marketing practices.

Marketing Results. If Vince Lombardi's statement, "Winning isn't everything-it's the only thing," is the consultant's watchword, this discussion is mute. Exhibit 9-2 shows that if winning is all that matters, ethics is irrelevant to procurement. Where ethics matter, however, the argument can be made that some stretching of ethical principles actually helps contract possibilities, and on some occasions is necessary to make a sale. This is true. However, the age-old question still persists: Do deception, exaggeration, lack of controls, and unethical justifications really achieve high results in the long run? There are two choices: One, the consultant accepts standard operating mores and proceeds to sustain an unfavorable advantage. He or she has little foresight and is not interested in developing much more. Two, the consultant sincerely believes that the quality of his or her work is measured by the results, the methods, and the process.

Consequences. Obviously, multiple possibilities exist, but let's examine three areas: consultant-centered, client-centered, and consultant-client interface.

Consultant-centered. First, the consultant should take a long, hard look at the current state of ethical practices. The examples listed in Exhibit 9-2 were for marketing operations, but by simple extrapolation all business operations can be reviewed. For instance, a group of consultants forms an ethics advisory group to identify unethical practices, monitor behavior, and recommend policy and disciplinary action. The policies are reviewed periodically to see where changes are needed.

Client-centered. Ethics are not a one-way street; they are guidelines for human behavior. Often clients are lax in responding to situations in a

EXHIBIT 9-2

Competitive Instances

Ethical Precept	Favorable Advantage	Unfavorable Advantage
Client interest ahead of consultant	Strives to resolve client issue	Wines and dines client
Confidentiality	Doesn't use client data in proposal	Uses client data to try to win proposal
Objectivity	Informs client of strengths and weaknesses	Leaves impression of high expertise in areas with little experience
Discovers client needs	Spends extra time understanding consulting tasks	Defines program for client
Equitable fees	Fees in direct proportion to resources used	Bids low to stifle competitors
Professional accomplishments	Discusses new approaches based on prior experience	Inflates achievements
Hiring client employees	Enacts firm policy giving time period before hiring	Revolving door
Open and honest results	Seeks critique and concurrence from client	Promises more than can deliver
Client contribution	Depends on client input to complete assignment	Will do anything necessary to make client look good
Nonprofessional inducements	Presents verifiable information only	Offers client perks if contract is let
Truthful qualifications	Modestly describes relevant experience	Include skills or experience had little to do with
Acceptance of engagement	Has proven track record or logical extension of past experience	Presents confident image even though client benefits unknown

Proposal submission	Creates readable, perceptive, realistic proposal which is cost effective	Shakes hands on oral agreement
Contingency fee	Refuses contingency fee	Requires contingency fee
Competing clients	States firm policy	Serves without mutual consent
Conflict of interest	Discloses any conflicts that may impair performance	Accepts contract even with conflict
Other client's consultants	Carefully defines involvement	Does whatever client asks
Client referrals	Refuses "finder's fee"	Accepts "finder's fee"
Hiring other consultants	Does so with consent of firm, at initiative of firm employee	Hires new consultant in order to win contract
Reporting unethical conduct	Affiliates with professional associations	Doesn't bother—could even hurt contract opportunities
Receiving inducements	Institutes firm policy not to subcontract or team with suppliers of services under contingency arrangements	Teams with suppliers so they will with us
Advertising services	Uses professional promotion methods	Uses formal and informal advertising freely

sensitive manner. Beyond this, however, is the fact that the client grants the contract. In recounting consultant abuses-needless contract extensions, cost overruns, lack of results, improper billing, excessive use of subcontractors-the *Post* dramatically illustrated how the procurement process was executed. Thus, the federal client must also bear responsibility for these practices.

The government must be willing to define the consultant need, use the results effectively, exercise controls on contract modifications or extensions, monitor spending} and prevent revolving-door abuses. To correct these deficiencies, the government needs to develop procedures that assure competition in the procurement process, justify the reasons for hiring an outside consultant and eliminate the potential duplication of effort. This undertaking will require several years, but steps can be taken now to reform the procurement process. The Office of Consulting Services, a new office in the Office of Personnel Management, assists other agencies with the procurement and evaluation of consulting services. Agency officials can use this office to increase the abilities of the contract team: the technical project officer, contract monitor, and senior managers. They can work with the office to ensure that the consultant's services are truly needed by the agency (that is) the tasks cannot be done in-house), are supported by upper management} and going to produce results that the agency is prepared to use. (See Chapter Ten for a complete description of contracting with the federal government.)

Consultant/client interface. If the consultant has become more ethically aware and the client uses controls that ensure fair competition, unreasonable or excessive fees should rarely occur. If a consultant bids on a project where there is a conflict of interest, the client should be able to site the potential conflict and reject the bid. If breaches of confidentiality, objectivity, or professional behavior occur, the client must be able to deal with the infractions in a expedient fashion. Consultant and client must be willing to work together for each other's mutual interest while sustaining a high degree of professional conduct.

Sample Task III

Drawing on your intuition and experience, answer the following questions:

1. Is consulting with another consultant during the course of a client engagement unethical? Why? Under what circumstances would it be done? Under what circumstances would it not be done? What impact does it have on the client/consultant relationship?
2. Regarding the following list of activities, do these acts breach an ethical code (such as Exhibit 9-1)? Why? What can a professional association do to modify such actions?
   a. Plagiarize material
   b. Tailor services by changing a few words in a "canned" approach
   c. Provide a finder's fee to a colleague for a referral leading to a contract

d. Lower agreed-to billing rate to gain competitive advantage
e. Extend services unnecessarily

DETERMINING YOUR LIABILITY

Consulting liability results from consultant negligence toward the client or client organization, and from client concerns due to errors, noncompliance with contract or statement of work, or unsatisfactory advice. Negligence results as much from poor communication as from substandard performance. Engineering consulting firms are concerned with liability; however, as this discussion will show, the principles and actions surrounding liability are potentially applicable to all types of consulting.

Today, the potential client is more aware of his or her legal rights in evaluating the quality of work being done. As a consequence, more malpractice claims have been filed against consultants than ever before. Sources of liability stem from:

- Failure to establish a trustworthy relationship with the client.
- Failure to schedule timely meetings to review the consulting activities.
- Failure to allow for disagreements.
- lack of a well-designed contract specifying the scope of work, its limits, contingencies, and responsibilities.
- Failure to adhere to professional ethics and association standards for a consulting assignment.
- lack of workable procedures for ensuring quality control and liability insurance.
- lack of sound judgment on the part of the consultant and on the part of the client.
- lack of procedures for resolving conflicts.

What can be done to reduce potential liability claims?

- Never perform work for the client without a clearly defined, written contract (see Chapter Five).
- Use a manual of procedures for performing standardized tasks, and perform work only in areas for which you are well qualified.
- Create an open, honest working relationship with the client and client staff, ensuring that schedules are met and tasks are done within budget.
- Develop contingency plans and funding; if necessary, carry liability insurance.

- Incorporate conflict resolution methods (including arbitration, mediation, committee consensus, or dialogue) in your service provision.
- Ensure that quality control procedures are carried out, and that effective performance reviews are done throughout the project.

All these precautions seek to limit malpractice suits from being filed. If a suit is brought against a consultant, settlement can occur through in-court or out-of-court means. The client's basic motivation is to collect damages. In most cases, the consulting contract could be written so that the potential liability incurred is limited to loss or damage that is *directly* attributable to the negligence. This guideline can take different forms in the contract.

Liability could be limited to:

1. The value of the consultant's fee.
2. A percentage of the consultant's fee.
3. A percentage of the total contract.
4. The amount of insurance coverage effected at the signing of the contract.
5. Direct damages, excluding consequential loss.

In addition, most contracts not only limit the amount for which the consultant can be held liable, but also the time of the liability. That is, a consultant will be responsible for only so many dollars of damages and only over a fixed time period.

Thus, how does a consultant decide what coverage to have for professional liability? This is an important decision. If you have few assets, carry no insurance. If a client sues, you will win or suffer minimal losses. On the other hand, if you do have assets or substantial income, malpractice insurance might be worthwhile. Because of the high cost and scarcity of malpractice insurance, it is suggested that you procure group coverage through an association or a pooling arrangement with your peers. As stated before, in lieu of malpractice insurance, liability amount and time could be stated in every contract and, if necessary, paid through normal business insurance. To select the appropriate kind and amount of insurance, consult with your lawyer and a carefully chosen or recommended insurance broker or agent. A clear understanding of your needs can be the key to effective contingency coverage.

Sample Task IV: Should Consultants Be Licensed?

Let's assume that a prospective consultant would take a standard examination administered by state officials. Upon successful completion, he or she would receive a license to practice consulting. Ask yourself the following questions:

- Would the procedure be required of all existing consultants?
- Can a "common" body of knowledge for consulting be devised?
- Can a consultant licensed in one state practice in others?
- How would standards of professional consulting practice be instituted and maintained?
- If you have a professional license, would you need another license to consult?
- Would certification by a consulting association be a more feasible substitute?
- Wouldn't licensing restrict those who can practice without expanding their quality of service options?

Case Example 9-1:

Client and Consultant Ethics: A Mirror Image

Goodkind and Associates, Inc., a social psychology consulting firm, was called in by a junior vice-president of Melbound Armatures Company. According to the junior vice-president, the morale in the company had never been worse. Employees were lethargic, disgusted, and disillusioned with management. The President of Goodkind, H.D. Goodkind, received permission to survey the employees to discover the underlying causes of their dissatisfaction. Goodkind's special skill is helping people feel at ease. He found that most employees were able to talk easily and honestly with him.

In previous situations, Goodkind had found that lack of attention, compensation, and advancement were major factors causing poor employee morale. This case was different. After interviewing 20 blue-collar workers and 10 managers, he concluded that employees were disgusted with the company's immoral behavior. Most employees felt uncomfortable about the unethical business dealings and the fact that top management condoned dishonest conduct.

The junior vice-president asked Goodkind for some examples. "Well," said Goodkind, "the activities cited are in part as follows:

- Padding the expense account
- Falsifying the time sheet
- Buying gifts for suppliers

- Overcharging the middleman
- Ignoring safety violations
- Withholding important information
- Conducting personal business on company time
- Using company equipment for personal reasons
- Deviating from company policies as a matter of course
- Firing whistle blowers
- Setting delivery dates two weeks earlier than actual shipment."

The junior vice-president was astonished. "It's hard for me to believe all this," he exclaimed. "I'm sure you are not the only one," said Goodkind. "Look, this is what I propose-to involve persons at all levels in the company in the exploration of why these situations exist and to determine whether they should be changed. To accomplish this I would like to hold a week-end retreat, focusing on ethics, with selected company representatives." The junior vice-president was all for it and got the other vice-presidents and the president to go along with the idea.

The weekend seminar was intense. It was designed to motivate the participants to uncover the causes of unethical behavior, to understand how such behavior damages employee morale, and to devise ways of countering such behavior. Here's what happened: Goodkind held an opening session in which he portrayed the company as acting in a Dr. Jekyll/Mr. Hyde mode, professing one thing and doing another. He then asked the participants to define ethics and ethical behavior; and then list ten examples of unethical behavior.

No one came up empty-handed. After writing the responses on large sheets of paper displayed at the front of the room, Goodkind went around and asked for causes and issues. He then divided the group into smaller working groups, each group taking three issues.

The next day was spent alternately in full session and small working groups. Each participant was attempting to understand how company policies foster less-than-ethical business conduct, how these policies (or lack of them) breed unethical behavior, and what steps could be taken to correct the situations. That evening Goodkind had volunteers act out various ethical situations to reinforce better ways of doing things.

On Sunday, each group was asked to develop long-term solutions to ethical behavior. The group chose the following topic areas:

- Personal ethics reminders
- Constructive communications
- Employee education

- Public awareness programs
- The advisability of an ethical code
- Reform of company policies
- Speak-out programs
- Punishment of ethical offenders

Each task force was to define its mission, suggest ways of achieving it, and devise an implementation plan. The entire group convened one last time to close the retreat. Goodkind warned them that ethical behavior "is the responsibility of each member of the firm. If you are not committed, the excitement of today will soon be replaced by the low morale of yesterday. But the steps taken here represent a giant stride toward more ethically sound operations."

Goodkind left the company with the mandate to review the ethical functions periodically to help ensure their viability.

Traveling back to his office, he realized how this company's ethical concerns are also his own. Yet, as a consultant, he considers ethics in each aspect of an assignment. For him, the company's problems represented the "tip of an ethical iceberg."

SUMMARY AND EXTENSION

This chapter has covered one of the more qualitative aspects of consulting-ethics. Ethical behavior is based on principles which when standardized form an ethical code. Application of such a code to private and public-sector consulting has proven to be successful. Yet, the short term versus long-term impact of such a code needs to be evaluated. Should the consultant merely focus on the immediate gains to be made without considering the spin-off effects on the client organization or on the public?

Should the consultant give the client what he or she wants today, or strive to attain what is needed for the long run? When implementing a solution to a client's problem, should the consultant gamble under the guise of a onetime, quick-turnaround venture, or take the risk of stressing the benefits in years to come? Or does the consultant have an obligation to report breaches of ethical conduct to his or her peers? These questions need to be considered by the consultant together with the other concerns raised in this chapter.

However, dealing successfully with all or any of these questions requires education. For example, at association conferences (see the Addendum for a comprehensive list), firm seminars, or university professional development programs, seminars on ethical concerns can be presented. Seminar participants could be encouraged to wrestle with the ethical issues, thereby furthering their own understandings. Such topics as enforcement and punishment, ethical relationships to other businesses, and different standards for different clients could be addressed.

Further, ethical insights also come from reflecting on various consulting experiences. But this act implies a willingness to interpret the ethical code you subscribe to, to glean honest and straightforward ways to handle a particular ethical concern or situation, and to keep the code viable. Being able to recognize and deal with ethical issues while carrying forth the consulting assignment is just as important as developing the other skills discussed in this book.

ADDENDUM: DIGEST OF CONSULTING ASSOCIATIONS

A list of many of the American consulting associations, institutes, and societies that serve various groups of consultants appears on the following pages. This addendum includes the type of organization with representative names; the address, phone number, and head of each organization; their founding dates, number of members, description of activities, and publications.[1] The list is necessarily incomplete because of the many ancillary organizations which have consultants as members but do not have "consulting" in the title. Nonetheless, an effort was made to include such groups in the list.

---

[1]Craig Cogate, Jr., *National Trade and Professional Associations,* 17th ed., Columbia Books, Inc., Washington, D.C., 1982; and Denise S. Akey, *Encyclopedia of Associations,* 17th ed., Vol. 1, Gale Research, Detroit, Mich., 1983.

Name	Address	Director	Founding Date	Membership	Description of Activities	Publications
A. Management Consultants						
Society of Professional Management Consultants (SPMC)	16 W. 56th St. New York, NY 10019 (212)586-2041	Paul Saunders	1959	125	Individuals engaged in providing business services who desire to establish and maintain professional and ethical standards in consulting. SPMC maintains referral service for public and private organizations and holds monthly seminars	*Professional Consultant* Registry of Accredited Professional Management Consultants
Project Management Institute (PMI)	P.O. Box 43 Drexel Hill, PA19026 (215)622-1796	James R.Snyder	1969	4,000	Individuals engaged in efforts to coordinate various disciplines to accomplish any desired project aim. Conducts programs on standards, intersociety liaison, education, career guidance, and research direction.	*PMI Quarterly* Proceedings and Special Reports

Organization	Address	Contact	Founded	Members	Description	Publications
Association of Internal Management Consultants (A IMC)	P.O. Box 472 Glastonbury, CT 06033 (203) 6335826	Thorne Perry	1971	175	Individuals engaged in developing the professional practice of internal management consulting by establishing performance standards, and serving as a forum for exchange of information, techniques, and interaction with client organizations.	*AIMC Newsletter* Membership Roster
Association of Management Consultants (AMC)	500 N. Michigan Ave. Chicago, IL 60611 (312)6611700	P.E. Hager	1959	110	Firms in management consulting subscribing to a code of professional practice and ethics. AMC operates client referral service and sponsors education programs.	*AMC Newsletter* Directory of Membership and Services
Institute of Management Consultants (IMC)	19 W. 44th St. New York, NY 10036 (212)9212885	John F. Hartshorne	1968	1,400	Individuals who become members through certification based on experience, ethical practice, and education. IMC sponsors conference seminars, and research on various aspects of management consulting.	*MC Newsletter* Directory

Name	Address	Director	Founding Date	Membership	Description of Activities	Publications
The Institute of Management Sciences (TIMS)	146 West minister St. Providence, RI02903 (401)2742525	M. R. DeMelim 1953	1953	6,000	Professional society for scientists, managers, and consultants. Aim is to advance scientific knowledge and improve management practices.	*Management Science OR/MS Today Interfaces Mathematics of Operation Research*
Professional and Technical Consultants Association (PATCA)	1190 Lincoln Ave. Suite 3 San Iose, CA 95125 (408)2878703	Jan Shepard	1975	225	Members are independent consultants. PATCA serves as marketing and networking referral service. Sponsors meetings for information exchange on monthly basis.	Directory
American Society for Training and Development (ASTD)	600 Maryland Ave.,S.W. Suite 305 Washington, DC20024 (202)4842390	Curtis E. Piatt	1944	25,000	Members are individuals engaged in the training and development of business, industrial, and government personnel. Conducts annual training institutes, compiles statistics, operates position referral service, undertakes special projects, has code of ethics	National Report Journal Exhibitor Newsletter Membership Directory Training Resources and Consultant Directory

Organization	Address	Contact	Founded	Members	Description	Publications
American Management Association (AMA)	135 W. 50th St. New York, NY 10020 (212)5868100	James L. Hayes	1923	91,000	Members are persons involved with management and management services. AMA provides educational, informational, communication; and development services worldwide. Has professional standards	*Compflash* Management Digest Management *Review SAM News International Supervisory Management Organizational Dynamics SAM Advanced Management Journal* Management Development Guide
American Institute of Certified Public Accountants (AICPA)	1211 Avenue of the Americas New York, NY 10036 (212)5756200	Philip B. Chenok	1887	**188,000**	Members are persons involved in providing accounting, auditing, or management advisory services (MAS) to various private and public clients. AICPA has division concerned with professional education, development ethics, and practices of those providing MAS	*CPA Letter Journal of Accountancy Tax Advisor*

Name	Address	Director	Founding Date	Membership	Description of Activities	Publications
Operations Research Society of America (ORSA)	428 E. Preston St. Baltimore, MD 21202 (301)5284146	Patricia H. Morris	1952	6,700	Members are persons interested in operations research in industry, government, and military applications. ORSA has code of ethics and professional practice, education programs, and technical research activities.	*Operations Research OR/MS Today Interfaces Directory*
Managerial Consultation Division, Academy of Management	Drawer Mg Mississippi State U. Mississippi State, MS 39762 (601)325-4944	Wilford G. Miles	1971	752	Most members are persons with a degree in business with a concentration in management. Area of focus is providing consulting assistance to managers. Other interests include extending theory and practice of consulting.	Division Newsletter Annual Meeting Proceedings Journal, Quarterly Review, Quarterly

Certified Consultants International (CCI)	Box 1625, Station B Nashville, TN 37235 (615)3224978	Edwin Bartee	1971	263	Established to certify consultants in four areas: (1) O.D., (2) Social Change, (3) Laboratory Education, and (4) Internal Organizational Development Consultant. Also assists clients in selection and use of consultants.	Newsletter Membership Directory
National Council of State Consultants in Elementary Education (NCSCEE)	State Dept. Education	J. Ronald West	1939	60	Individuals and state groups responsible for elementary education. NCSCEE seeks to acquaint and extend services of U.S. Office of Education to members.	Newsletter *Planning for American Children*

Name	Address	Director	Founding Date	Membership	Description	Publications
B. Business Consultants						
Association of Executing Recruiting Consultants(AERC)	30 Rockefeller Plaza New York, NY 10020 (212)5417580	James G. Gonzelman	1959	60	Executive search firms specializing in recruiting management personnel for client companies. AERC members must meet strict membership requirements and are pledged to follow a professional code of ethics	
National Association of Pension Consultants and Administrators (NAPCA)	1432 Duke St. Alexandria, VA 22314 (703)6840180	David Strachan	1960	2,400	Members are private employment agencies. Compiles statistics on professional agency growth and development. Conducts certification program for all members.	*Personnel Consultant* Directory

National Personnel Consultants (NPC)	535 Court St. P.O. Box 1379 Reading, PA 19603 (215)3768486	John Weir	1935	80	Members are employment agencies engaged in intercity, cooperative placement of personnel in administrative, marketing, and technical categories.	*The Employment Counselor*
National Association of Personnel Consultants(NAPC)	Three Piedmont Center Suite 300 Atlanta, GA 30342 (404)2310100	John W. Baker	1974	500	Members are individuals and firms that are pension planners and consultants. NAPCA initially organized to help its members comply with ERISA.	*NAPCA Newsletter*

Name	Address	Director	Founding Date	Membership	Description	Publications
Association of Tax Consultants (ATC)	2433 N.E. Clarkamas St.Portland, OR 97232 (503)2491040	Bill Bogan	1972	800	ATC seeks to (1) develop professional standards through continuing education and code of ethics, (2) protect the rights of tax practitioners, (3) establish local control through state legislatures, (4) monitor licensing and consumer protection laws and tax reforms, and (5) assist members with job search.	Tax *Times* Membership Roster
National Association of Financial Consultants (NAFC)	2950 S. Jamaica Ct. Suite 302Aurora, CO 80014 (303)7508868	Robert W. Fisher	1976	175	Members are professional financial consultants working with companies and individuals to secure financing for commercial projects.	*The Financial Consultant*

						Newsletter Membership Directory
National Association of Merger and Acquisition Consultants (NAMAC)	2241 Valwood Pkwy Dallas, TX 75234 (214)241-0254	Joe M. Leonard, Jr.	1973	55	Members are individuals highly skilled and meeting NAMAC criteria of professional competence. NAMAC role is promotion of education, enhancement of image of merger/acquisition specialists, and confidential information distribution on available merger or aquisition prospects.	
Institute of Personal Image Consultants	c/o Editorial Services Company 1140 Avenue of the Americas 10th Floor	Jacqueline A. Thompson	1978	250	Information clearing house serving the personal image consulting profession. Comprised of practitioners engaged in	Directory

Name	Address	Director	Founding Date	Membership	Description	Publications
	New York, NY 10036 (212) 3545025				speech and public appearance coaching, dress coordination and selection, and personal public relations counseling. Established to advance the interest of the industry and to publicize its services	
Institute of Risk Management Consultants (IRMC)	58 Diablo View Dr. Orinda, CA 94104 (415)2549472	David Warren	1975	60	Clearinghouse for services to clients needing analysis of risk potentials	*The Communicator*

Association	Address	Contact	Founded	Members	Description	Publications
Association of Productivity Specialists (APS)	200 Park Ave. Suite 303E New York, NY 10166 (212)2860943	Albert B. Dorr	1977	150	Members are companies and individuals engaged in performance improvement using productivity methods. Has certification programs.	Newsletter *Productivity Monitor* Salary and Fringe Benefits Survey
Internationl Association of Strategic Planning Consultants (IASPC)	Box 5198 Akron, OH 44313 (216)8368685	Ivan Boyd	1979	180	Companies and individuals serving clients in the fields of corporate, new venture, or strategic planning. IASPC promotes standards of consultant performance, has client referral services, sponsors surveys, conducts research, and offers educational programs.	*Strategies* Directory
International Association of Book Publishing Consultants	485 Fifth Ave. New York, NY 10017 (212)8676341	Joseph Marks				

Name	Address	Director	Founding Date	Membership	Description	Publications
Professional Services Council (PSQ)	1730 Pennsylvania Ave., N.W. Suite 1200 Washington, DC **20006** (202)2233835	Virginia Littlejohn	1972	156	Firms that participate in contracting with the federal government for consulting services. Role of PSC is advocacy, lobbying, and public relations to secure stronger public support and greater contracting.	
American Association of Political Consultants (AAPC)	1101 N. Calvert St. Suite 1406 Baltimore, MD 21202 (301)5398555	Phyllis B. Brotman	1969	154	Members are individuals engaged in political counseling. AAPC provides for exchange of information and seminars on media use, campaign financing, and computer use.	Directory

Association of Graphic Arts Consultants (AGAC)	Printing Industries of America 1730 N. Lynn St. Arlington, VA 22209 (703)841-8140	Edward W. Hill, Jr	1976	50	Members are individuals with B.A. degree and at least two years' experience in graphic arts. AGAC sponsors seminars and management audit programs.	Directory *Printing Mergers and Acquisition News*
International College of Real Estate Consulting Professionals (RECP)	305 Foshay Tower Minneapolis, MN 55402 (507)3327903	D.M. Pexa	1972	333	Members are individuals proficient in areas of real estate. ACREC has certification program for membership, conducts seminars, maintains library, compiles statistics, and maintains placement and referral services.	Newsletter Journal Digest Directory

Chapter Ten

Consulting for the Public Sector

SNAPSHOT

Until now, we have assumed that if you are consulting, it must be for a private concern. This chapter and the following one take a thorough look at the differences in performing services for the public sector-specifically, the federal government-and for a foreign client. In these chapters the following assumptions are made:

- The federal government examples can be used for doing business with state or local government.
- The foreign client example discussed holds in most countries.
- Consulting for the government or a foreign country tends to be more formal and complex, and it requires a great deal of documentation.

Yet, if you understand the procurement process and the needed services, the contracts will be yours.

MARKETING THE FEDS: STRATEGY OR LUCK?

The majority of government contracts are awarded through a formal competitive procurement procedure. To locate government prospects, you can communicate with agency administrators, program directors, or project managers. You can concentrate on one agency or similar departments of several agencies. And you can bid on large, medium-size, or small awards that last

---

EXHIBIT 10-1

Federal Marketing Approach

1. Define services
2. Depict current market
3. Detail plausible federal areas
4. Gather information about client/service match
5. Relate marketing activity to overall marketing goals
6. Ascertain marketing leads
7. Gain client entry
8. Evaluate the prospective contract
9. Decide on contract tactics
10. Bid
11. Review contracting effort
12. Engage in follow-up activities
13. Modify your approach
14. Seek future contracts

---

anywhere from six months to five years. Whatever the combination of factors, you must see a direct correlation between your skills and the client's needs. Thus your approach must be targeted, as illustrated in Exhibit 10-1.

1. *Define services.* As a consultant, you possess a range of skills and tools. List your skills and specify your prior successes and failures.
2. *Depict current market.* Where are your services currently being used? What is the potential for future growth among your current clients? Are you currently using skills that could be transferred to a federal client? Do these skills have potential for future growth among your clients?
3. *Detail plausible federal areas.* Does the government need your services? Where are the needs to be found, and why? Who are the people to contact in each federal area, and how might you locate them?
4. *Gather information about client! service match.* Find out where the demand for your services is greatest. Decide which services you wish to market to the federal government, and why.
   Marketing the Feds: Strategy or Luck? / 167
5. *Relate to overall marketing goals.* Match your federal marketing strategy with your other marketing activities. Also, become familiar with the federal procurement process.

6. *Ascertain marketing leads.* Study several agencies and agency officials, and narrow the list to those you can pursue to the contract signing stage.
7. *Gain client entry.* Test the market. Using the methods described in Chapter Four, try to get through the prospective client door. Find out the client's interest and devise a way to secure a contract.
8. *Evaluate the prospective contract.* Tell the client what your strengths and weaknesses are in fulfilling the contract. Note the response.
9. *Decide on contract tactics.* How many contracts will you bid on? What form will the contracts be (fixed price, unsolicited, and so forth)? When is the award date? What is the dollar amount and special provisions of the contract?
10. *Bid.* Submit a proposal for each potential contract. Respond to all elements of the Request for Proposals (RFP), if one exists. Spend ample time constructing and composing your proposal. Be prepared for oral competition and negotiation. Draw on your prior experience in moving the proposal to the final qualifying stage. Do not underbid, but be prepared to justify costs (see Chapter Eight).
11. *Review contracting effort.* Win or lose, critique your performance on this marketing endeavor. Note changes in marketing, ways to make these changes, and when they will occur.
12. *Engage in follow-up activities.* If you do not win the contract, meet with the client to discuss future opportunities, including using consulting "products" (see Chapter Seven).
13. *Modify your approach.* Keep abreast of federal contracting personnel changes. Attempt to merge your federal marketing plans into your overall marketing strategy. Develop more finely tuned marketing skills and establish long-term relationships with federal clients through direct contract experience and professional activities.
14. *Seek future contracts.* Continue to build your reputation one contract at a time. Search for federal contract work, avoid entrenchment, and be versatile in marketing various federal sectors with your services. This step-by-step approach to find and sustain new clients and to discover additional clients can make the difference between successful marketing and failure. Marketing is not an exact science, but your results can be enhanced if you use common sense and systematic techniques.

Sample Task I

For a solo practitioner, a wise marketing strategy for the federal sector is to sell skills as a subcontractor since the costs are less. Comment on these remarks.

UNDERSTANDING FEDERAL PROCUREMENT

The federal government is one of the largest consumers in the United States. It demands three types of goods or services: old or new technology; facilities and supplies; and management services and training. The greatest demand for consultants comes in this last category. The federal government has used consultants because it has traditionally been less expensive and faster to have an outside contractor do the job. Consulting with the government is a formal process, based on supplying goods and services in support of government activities. It is fraught with paperwork and compliance with specific procedures, and it is subject to technical review and monetary auditing.

Consultants can be involved in both grant and contract procurements, which are compared in Exhibit 10-2. Most consultants will not apply for

---

EXHIBIT 10-2
Grants and Contracts: A Comparison

Characteristic	*Grant*	*Contract*
Definition	An award, based on legislation, that enables a program to be carried out independently of federal involvement	An award, not usually based on legislation, that enables a federal agency's program to be carried out with the assistance of the recipient
Eligibility	Nonprofit organizations only (with rare exception)	Unrestricted (unless otherwise specified)
Solicitation document	Program announcement	Request for Proposals(RFP)
Major document source	Federal Register or Catalog of Federal Domestic Assistance	Commerce Business Daily
Number of awards	Multiple	Single
Follow-up	Cyclical renewal	Not usually
Payment schemes	Cost reimbursement Cost sharing	Fixed price Cost plus, fixed price Basic ordering agreement

Subcontracting	Unrestricted (unless Unrestricted otherwise specified)	(unless otherwise specified)
Deliverables	Generally, a report produced at end of award period; not required for payment	Produced at intervals during award period; required for payment
Schedule of payments	Quarterly, in advance	Monthly or quarterly, after costs incurred
Technical monitoring	Minimal	Regular
Financial control	Flexible; little auditing	Strict; closely audited

grants directly due to the nonprofit restriction, the inability to make a profit, and the requirement of having a program in need of federal assistance. [However, in certain instances, such as for research, federal agencies will award a grant to a profit-making firm. Again, the grant will cover expenses with no provision(s) for a profit.] It would be more likely for a consultant to act as a subcontractor to the grant recipient, providing technical skills and management services agreed upon in the subcontract. For these reasons, the subsequent three sections will focus on contract awards.

The federal government requests consulting services by a formal solicitation, a Request for Proposals (RFP). A main source for discovering potential new business is the *Commerce Business Daily,* which announces all proposed contracts in excess of $10,000, and all recently awarded contracts of $25,000 and up. Another way to find out about RFPs is to have your name put on a bidder's list. You can obtain a bidder's list application from any federal procurement office. After you fill out the application and file it with a procurement office, your name is added to the list and when a relevant RFP is released, a copy is automatically sent to you. There are a number of problems with this procedure. First, if your interests are broad, you might have to file a number of forms with different offices. Second, the bidder's lists are not kept up to date or matched well with the RFPs. Third, when a RFP is sent, the procurement officials expect the interested party to respond.

If two or three RFPs are sent to you and you do not respond, your name could be dropped from the list. Additional ways to learn of currensolicitations and proposed procurements are described in Exhibit 10-3.

EXHIBIT 10-3

Sources of Contract Information

Types of References	*Name*	*Frequency*	*Contents*	*Availability*
Periodicals	*Commerce Business Daily*	Monday-Friday	Basic data on most potential and warded contracts	Supt. of Documents U.S. Government Printing Office Washington, DC 20402
	Federal Contracts Report	Weekly	Major developments in government contracting	Bureau of National Affairs Washington, DC 20037
	The Government Contractor	Biweekly	Reports and analyses of significant government contract rulings and regulations	Federal Publications, Inc. Washington, DC 20006
	Government Marketing News	Monthly	Discusses trends, prospects, and new developments in procuring government contracts	Government Marketing News Washington, DC 20006
	Federal Register	Monday-Friday	Report guidelines and regulations for government programs	Supt. of Documents U.S. Government Printing Office Washington, DC 20402

	Government Contracts Reports	Weekly	Developments in federal procurement	Commerce Clearinghouse Washington, DC 20004
	Contracting Appeals Decisions	Biweekly	Texts of contracted appeals from 12 agencies	Same as above
Books and reports	*Anyone Can Do Business with the Government*		A Current step-by-step guide to contracting with the federal government	Government Marketing News Washington, DC 20036
	Guide to Federal Assistance Programs for Minority Business	Yearly	Explains procedures for obtaining contracts and loans from government agencies	Dept. of Commerce, CMBE Washington, DC 20230
	U.S. Government Manual	Yearly	Guidebook about U.S. government agencies, programs, and key officials	Supt. of Documents U.S. Government Printing Office Washington, DC 20402
	Sources of Information for Selling to the Federal Government	Editions	Handbook for domestic, congressional, and informational contracting	Washington Researchers Washington, DC 20006

Programs	Small Business Administration (SBA)	Ongoing	Training, loan and loan guarantees, contract set-asides, minority firm set-asides, certification and location services for small businesses	SBA 1441 L Street, N.W. Washington, DC 20416 (and regional offices)
	Economic Development Administration (EDA)	Ongoing	Grants and loans or loan guarantees to private businesses	Department of Commerce EDA Washington, DC 20230
	Office of Minority Business Enterprise (CMBE)	Ongoing	Contracts to organizations to, in turn, provide technical assistance to training to minority owned firms	Department of Commerce OMBE Washington, DC 20230
	Business Service Centers	Ongoing	Counseling and information about doing business with the federal government	General Services Administration 18th and F Streets, N.W. Washington, DC 20405 (congressional offices)
	Training	Twice yearly	Seminars on various aspects of government contracting	Federal Publications, Inc. Washington, DC 20006

Preaward Information	Daily	RFP summaries and proposal notes for most federal agencies	Washington Representative Services Arlington, VA 22203

If you desire a copy of the solicitation, write to the contracting officer. Exhibit 10-4 describes the contents of an RFP. The elements in an RFP might vary, but make sure that all of them are there; if anything is missing, contact the contracting officer.

Most RFPs are issued 6 to 12 weeks before proposals are due. Awards are usually made one to four months after the proposal has been submitted.

EXHIBIT 10-4

The Elements of a RFP

Part	*Function*
Cover sheet	Gives title, RFP number, contracting officer, issuing agency, due date, place for delivery and contact
Standard Form 33	Is letter to bid with
Offerer representations and certificates	Ensure compliance with business, labor, environment, job, foreign, etc., regulations States conditions of the proposal
Solicitation provisions and conditions	Informs bidders about preproposal conference, proprietary information, patent and copyright policies, and default conditions
General instructions	Describes specifications of proposal response, number of copies to submit, and exceptions to response procedure; evaluation factors are also stated
Statement of work	Details type of technical content proposal response should have
Billing instructions	States means and frequency of contract payment

A preproposal conference could be held, depending on the amount of the procurement and the agency. This meeting is usually held at a government facility with the contracting officer and project manager there to clarify the RFP, answer questions, and give any additional information on the procurement.

After reviewing the RFP, you must decide whether to bid on the proposal or decline. This decision can be made without attending the preproposal conference, although information received there could be useful. To gain a sense of the risks and values in responding, ask yourself the following questions:

- Can the proposal be responded to on time?
- Is there the management/staff capability to bid?
- Is there the management/staff capability to execute the contract?
- Will this contract further my company's objectives?
- How knowledgeable am I about the potential client organization?
- Are any of my ideas in the RFP?
- What kind of competition am I likely to face? Is the contract "wired"?
- Can I use a proven strategy to service this client?
- How expensive is it to respond to the RFP?

Most consulting proposals outline the means of addressing a client issue and the costs (as discussed in Chapter Five). Exhibit 10-5 illustrates how to efficiently and quickly generate a competitive proposal for a government contract.

The basic substance of the RFP's response is the technical proposal. The form varies, but the questions are standard:

- Who is the client, what is creating the issue, and briefly, what is the issue?
- What kind of approach will resolve the issue?
- How will the consultant coordinate the resources necessary to carry out the approach?
- When will the results begin to appear, and what will they be?
- What prior experience and qualifications does the consultant have for performing this assignment?

A technical proposal is generally designed as follows:

Introduction. This section sets the stage, describing the client's situation, the factors that created the issue, and the client's current understanding of the issue. Also, any previous work by other consultants or clients is noted.

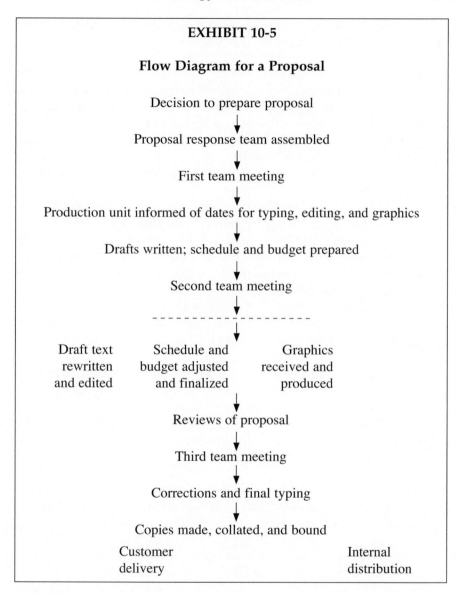

EXHIBIT 10-5

Flow Diagram for a Proposal

Decision to prepare proposal

Proposal response team assembled

First team meeting

Production unit informed of dates for typing, editing, and graphics

Drafts written; schedule and budget prepared

Second team meeting

- - - - - - - - - - - - - - - - - - - -

| Draft text rewritten and edited | Schedule and budget adjusted and finalized | Graphics received and produced |

Reviews of proposal

Third team meeting

Corrections and final typing

Copies made, collated, and bound

Customer delivery   Internal distribution

Technical approach. Herein the method to be employed to resolve the issue is detailed. Reasons for using this method are stated in terms of how well it will resolve the issue compared to other methods. Each step is explained fully together with the benefits to be derived and results to be delivered.

Management plan. In this portion, all resources are listed and their use in this project is explained. Such items include:

1. *Project organization and staff.* The personnel involved in this project are noted on a management chart, as well as the facilities and resources. Each project team member's responsibilities are described together with the ways in which the team will interact with the client.

   The type of consultant quality control system, any special provisions, or contingencies are also mentioned.

2. *Schedules and deliverables.* Two charts are included here: the Gantt and PERT charts. The Gantt chart shows the time sequence for the tasks and subtasks described in the Technical Approach. In horizontal bar form, it demonstrates how much time is needed to perform each function. The PERT chart displays the involvement of each staff member in the project.

   Again, in horizontal bar form it shows who will perform each technical function. There is also another Gantt chart for client meetings, status reports, and all other deliverables.

3. *Experience and qualifications.* Any relevant experience is stated here. The size of the organization, the skills of the staff, and the company's physical facilities and location are all described.

Besides these essential proposal elements, there are other items that are generally included:

- A transmittal letter to the prospective client that expresses interest in the project.
- A cover sheet for the document, a table of contents page, and a list of illustrations.
- A foreword or preface acknowledging an interest in the client initiated effort and a match between the client needs and the consultant's abilities.
- Appendices that include materials related to the proposal.

All technical proposals for the government contain a notice that restricts the use of the information presented to the procurement office, thus safeguarding proprietary information. The cost proposal is composed on Optional Form 60 (using the cost factors and payment schemes mentioned in Chapter Eight). An example is given in Exhibit 10-6. This form is mailed or delivered with original and multiple copies to the office designated by the appropriate date. In general, it is difficult to discuss the procurement with federal program officials during the proposal-writing phase, unless expressly permitted by the contracting officer. It is extremely important to respond to all of the questions

EXHIBIT 10-6

CONTRACT PRICING PROPOSAL (RESEARCH AND DEVELOPMENT)		Office of Management and Budget Approval No 29-RO184	
This form is for use when (i) submission of cost or pricing data (see FPR 1-3.807-3) is required and (ii) substitution for the Optional Form 59 is authorized by the contracting officer.		PAGE NO.	NO OF PAGES
NAME OF OFFEROR		SUPPLIES AND/OR SERVICES TO BEFURNISHED	
HOME OFFICE ADDRESS			
DIVISION(S) AND LOCATION(S) WHERE WORK IS TO BE PERFORMED		TOTAL AMOUNT OF PROPOSAL	GOV'T SOLICITA-TION NO.
DETAIL DESCREPTION OF COST ELEMENTS			
1. DIRECT MATERIAL		EST COST	TOTAL EST COST	REFER-ENCE
a. PURCHASED PARTS			
b. SUBCONTRACTED ITEMS			
1. OTHER – (i) RAW MATERIAL			
(ii) YOUR STANDARD COMMERCIAL ITEM			

		ESTIMATED HOURS	RATE/ HOUR	EST COST(S)		
(iii) INTERDIVISIONAL TRANSFERS (A: other item cost)						
2. MATERIAL OVERHEAD'						
3. DIRECT LABOR (Specify)						
TOTAL DIRECT LABOR						
4. LABOR OVERHEAD (Specify Department or Cost Center)	O.H. RATE	K SASE=		EST COST(S)		
TOTAL LABOR OVERHEAD						
5. SPECIAL TESTING (Iicluding field work as Government installations				EST COST (S)		

		EST CODT (S)	
TOTAL SPECIAL TESTING			
6. SPECIAL EQUIPMENT (if direct charge) (itemize on Exhibit A)			
7. TRAVEL (Iff direct charge) (Give details on aswebed Schedule)			
a. TRANSPORTATION			
b. PER DIEM OR SUBSISTENCE			
TOTAL TRAVEL			
8. CONSULTANTS (Identify- purpose- rate)			
TOTAL CONSULTANTS			
9. OTHER DIRECT COST (Itenize on Exhibit A)			
10.			
11. GENERAL AND ADMINISTRATIVE EXPENSE (Rate % of cost rlement Nos.			
12. ROYALTIES			
13. TOTAL ESTIMATED COST			
14. FEE OR PROFIT			
TOTAL ESTIMATED COST AND FEE OR PROFIT			

This proposal is submitted for are in connection with and in response to (Describe RFP. etc.) and reflects our bese estimates as of this date. in accotdence with the instructions to Offerors and the Foot-notes which follow.

TYPED NAME AND TITLE	SIGNATURE	
NAME OF FIRM		DATE OF SUBMISSION

EXHIBIT A – SUPPORTING SCHEDULE (Specify. If more space is needed. use reserse)

COST EL NO.	ITEM DESCRIPTION (SEE FOOTNOTE 5)	EST COST(S)

I. HAS ANY EXECUTIVE AGENCY OF THE UNITED STATES GOVERNMENT PERFORMED ANY REVIEW OF YOUR ACCOUNTS OR RECORDS IN CONNECTION WITH ANY OTHER GOVERNMENT PRIME CONTRACT OR SUBCONTRACT WITHIN THE PAST TWELVE MONTHS?

YES ☐   NO ☐   (if yes, identify below)

NAME AND ADDRESS OF REVIEWING OFFICE AND INDIVIDUAL	TELEPHONE NUMBER/EXTENSION

II. ALL YOU REQUIRE THE USE OF ANY GOVERNMENT CONTRACT FINANCING TO PERFORM THIS PROPOSED CONTRACT

☐ YES   ☐ NO

III. DO YOU REQUIRE GOVERNMENT CONTRACT FINANCING TO PERFORM THIS PROPOSED CONTRACT ☐

IV. DO YOU NOW HOLD ANY CONTRACT (Or, do you have any independenify finaneed (IR&D) projects) FOR THE SAME OR SINILAR WORK CALLED FOR BY THIS PROPOSED CONTRACT? ☐

V. DOSE THIS COST SUMMARY CONFORM WITH THE COST PRINCIPLES SET FORTH IN AGENCY REGULATIONS? ☐

in the RFP. Inclusion of schedules that differ from the instructions, or a late response, can lead to disqualification.

However, one way to modify the scope of work presented in the RFP is to respond to the RFP according to the instructions and include sections showing your modifications and reasons for them. Minor exceptions could be left for the negotiation phase.

The evaluation of submitted responses to an RFP is complex and differs among federal agencies. But there are some standard rules:

- The proposal is generally evaluated in two separate parts: the technical and the cost.
- One or more committees review(s) the proposals.
- A rating system is used to rank responses.
- The contracting officer or, in some instances for large awards, a senior official makes the final determination.

As shown in Exhibit 10-7, at the beginning of the procurement, committees are formed to oversee the solicitation. The administration committee normally determines the factors to be used in assessing the proposal responses. The evaluation factors for award need to be published as part of the RFP. After all the responses to the RFP have been received, the technical committee, using formulated weighting criteria, assesses the technical worthiness of the proposal. Such criteria are developed by each federal agency. Exhibit 10-8 shows a sample scoring scheme. In Exhibit 10-9, this scheme is applied to a hypothetical evaluation. The technical committee reports on each proposal, justifying how each factor was ranked, listing the ambiguities requiring attention, and summarizing the proposal.

Since the evaluation scheme is described in the RFP, the consultant can focus his or her effort in two ways. First, the technical proposal can stress those items given the highest score, or the consultant can try to gain an advantage for those items which he or she feels are likely to vary the most in points given. Such tactics can help you submit a proposal with a favorable competitive edge.

A business or cost committee examines the cost portion of the proposal. The rating is usually not too elaborate: a (+) is noted for superior cost features, a (-) for inferior costs features, and a (v) for features in the range of success.

The best way to submit a successful bid is not to underbid, but to be realistic about your costs-expenditures that will enable you to execute the work efficiently and punctually. In addition, the business committee will verify whether the cost estimates correlate with the agency's guidelines.

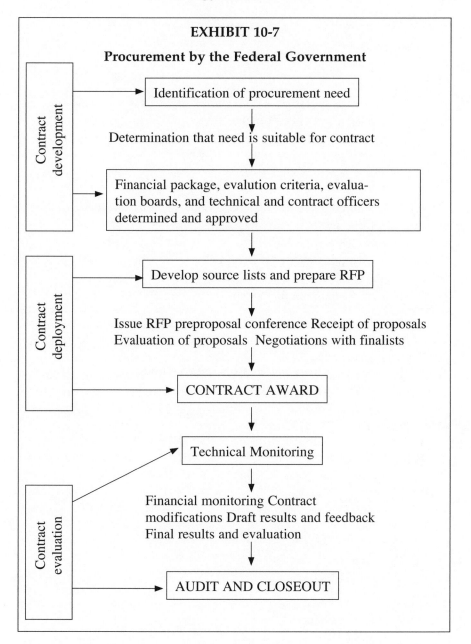

EXHIBIT 10-7

Procurement by the Federal Government

Contract development

Identification of procurement need

Determination that need is suitable for contract

Financial package, evelution criteria, evaluation boards, and technical and contract officers determined and approved

Contract deployment

Develop source lists and prepare RFP

Issue RFP preproposal conference Receipt of proposals Evaluation of proposals Negotiations with finalists

CONTRACT AWARD

Technical Monitoring

Contract evaluation

Financial monitoring Contract modifications Draft results and feedback Final results and evaluation

AUDIT AND CLOSEOUT

EXHIBIT 10-8

Proposal Scoring Scheme

Value	*Meaning*	*Action*
0.0-0.4	Factor or subfactor is deficient in management ability, engineering, or scientific judgment. If, however, the proposal is selected for further negotiations, such deficiencies can be corrected.	List weaknesses
0.4-0.6	Factor or subfactor is ambiguous. Offerer needs to clarify in written or oral discussions.	List unclear points
0.6-1.0	Factor or subfactor is understood. However, discussions involving such elements are not precluded.	No commentary or list strengths

---

EXHIBIT 10-9

Proposal Evaluation Method

Factor	*Weight (Set Forth in RFP)*	*Scoring Scheme*	*Actual Weight (for This Proposal)*
1. Adequacy of technical proposal	50	0.9	45
a. Understanding of the problem	15		10
b. Soundness of the technical approach	25		25
c. Adequate review of literature	5		5
d. Clearly defined and presented products	5		5
2. Project management	30	0.5	15
a. Previous experience with topic	10	0.0	0
b. Soundness of project organizing and planning	10		10
c. Degree of proposed transition, debriefing, and follow-up	10	0.5	5

3. Personnel qualifications	20	0.45	9
a. Past experience with client	7	0.0	0
b. Technical experience of offeoer	7		5
c. Educational qualifications	3		3
d. Intensity of outside support	3	0.3	1
Total	100		69

Then the results from the three committees are given to the government official in charge of administering the contract. In turn, this contracting officer will ask the bidders for clarifications or revisions as required.

Then a small number of finalists are chosen and often are asked to make oral presentations to reaffirm their ability to do the work and to negotiate the cost proposal. After these orals, winners are chosen.

Those respondents who were unsuccessful in obtaining a contract may request a debriefing, where the contracting officer or associate will review the proposal's evaluation and explain why the successful proposal was chosen. The debriefing can reveal qualitative aspects of the procurement process that could help the potential contractor win another procurement.

No confidential information or techniques are revealed.

Different types of contracts can be negotiated: fixed price, cost plus fee, time and materials, or variations (see Chapter Five). Before the contract is awarded, an internal survey of the consultant's organization is made to access the solvency and efficacy of the business. Such surveys can be drudgery or an opportunity depending on the consultant's attitude. In most cases, the auditors will find minor infractions of the federal rules. Practically speaking, these infractions are unavoidable given the complexity and vagueness of procurement procedures. Yet many times auditors recommend contract controls that save the consultant future headaches.

Finally, how can inexperienced or small firms successfully obtain government business? We already mentioned straight, competitive submittal or subcontracting to a contractor as common means. Also, joint collaboration with such firms could be a feasible option, as each group can pool skills in presenting a multicompetent team to carry out the effort successfully.

Sample Task II

What are the primary costs of proposing? Use the cost-control techniques in Chapter Eight to discover ways to reduce these costs.

When a consultant enters into a contractual agreement with the federal government, it is to perform support services. Thus the consultant becomes, in government jargon, "a support service contractor." By contrast, a government consultant is an individual who is hired on a temporary assignment within a federal agency to give direct advice to operating personnel of that agency.

OBTAINING THE CONTRACT

Support contracts can be extended or modified by means that are generally described in the solicitation. Some awards are targeted for small, disadvantaged, minority, or woman-owned firms. Also, there is a slightly more expeditious procedure for contract award and payment for procurements of $10,000 or less. In some cases, support contracts are given on a sole-source or unsolicited basis. This type of contract emerges from discussions with people in the agency. Sole-source discussions are initiated by the client, in the belief that a consulting firm is best qualified to do the work.

Unsolicited discussions are initiated by the consulting firm that has a unique idea for client use. Together, contractor and contractee define the type of assistance needed by the agency, what is required immediately, and for which the consultant is uniquely qualified. The consultant submits a less formal technical response than with an RFP and includes a standard cost form. The contract can be signed through a letter agreement within a short period of time, providing an expedient means of dealing with the client's situation.

Usually, the procurement office decides what kind of RFP to use and whether a proposed scope of work can be approved as a sole-source contract. Procurement procedures vary from agency to agency. Some agencies have central procurement offices, others have an office for almost every division. Contracting officers together with appointed agency administrators set the procurement activities; others delegate authority to program or project managers. Some agencies will issue many sole-source contracts; other agencies will generally award competitive procurements to the low bidder; and still others will never make unsolicited awards.

Yet there are only a few fundamental instances that could nullify an awarded contract. One way is if the contractor changes the agreement without informing the contracting officer in the specified time frame and manner, or if the contractor fails to perform support services in the contracted time period.

Another way is if an unsuccessful bidder contests the award and files a protest with the General Accounting Office (GAO).

The GAO will then investigate the matter and have it adjudicated. If the court finds in favor of the plaintiff, the award is overturned and it could be reawarded to the plaintiff. This protest option stimulates an environment of fairness. A fourth way is "termination of convenience." The federal government may wish to abort a contract when the product is no longer considered of value. This contract clause may also be used to revoke a portion of a contract rather than the total procurement. If a contract is terminated in this fashion, the contractor is entitled to a settlement. When the contractor accepts the settlement, the contract or contract portion ends. After negotiations, if the contractor feels that the settlement is not equitable, adjudication may be used.

Also, provisions are specified in each contract for modifications, extensions, revisions, and subcontracting. Whenever the technical project manager and contractor agree, any of these mechanisms may be invoked beyond the original contracted provisions in order to complete the scope of work or a revised scope of work. Further, the GAO can audit selected contracts to evaluate the management of particular agency programs.

Requests for such audits come from members of Congress or congressional committees. Such audits can occur up to three years after final payment of the contract. The contractor is informed of the audit's results, which generally include disclosure of all documents and records dealing with cost accounting data. The GAO then submits a final report to the contracting agency and to the Congress. Over the years, such audits have been done with increasing frequency.

Sample Task III

The real cause of the present federal procurement predicament is lack of leadership. If the contract officers and technical managers would "get tough" with their needs analysis, the contractors would have to demonstrate before award rather than after. Is this action plausible? Why?

Sample Task IV

Which of the following describes the best approach to take in contracting with the federal government for consulting services? Justify your choice.

- Exploit and manipulate contract regulations to full advantage.
- Play strictly by the rules.

- Learn the procurement system of the specific agency and know what to expect during the procurement stages.
- Decline to submit a proposal due to a faulty work statement and report this to the contracts administrator.
- All of the above and more.

CONSULTING WITH OTHER PUBLIC-SECTOR CLIENTS

The major emphasis in this chapter has been on the federal government the largest purchaser of consulting services. However, state, county, and city governments also retain such services. In the following discussion, county and city are labeled "municipal" Exhibit 10-10 describes the differences in

---

EXHIBIT 10-10

Contrasts in Consulting among Government Clients

Consulting Variable	Federal	State	Municipal
Issue publicity	Published in CBD	Sometimes announcements in state periodicals Informal communication channels	Word of mouth and past experience predominate
Issue definition	Formal procedure	Combination of formal and in formal procedures	Informal procedure
Solicitation process	Response to RFP	RFP or letter bid	Qualifications statement, letter, bid, or RFP
Contract jusification	Required of all procurements	Suggested for procurements	Optional
Consultant selection	Committee procedures	By committee or official	Through comments of officials

---

Contract terms	Fixed beforehand	Fixed at time of award	Fixed at time of signing the contract
Monitoring	Procedures do exist	Few mechanisms	Hardly any
Evaluation	Occasionally	Infrequently	Rarely
Implementation	Variable and partially documented	Variable and partially documented	Variable and partially documented

issues and procedures among these clients. As we mentioned, the majority of federal contracts are found in the Commerce *Business Daily*.

This practice is carried out in a piecemeal fashion at the state level and rarely at the local level. For contracts under $10,000 or sole-source procurements, preaward announcements are rarely made. State and municipal clients are not as interested as the federal client in ensuring that service contracts are met competitively. This is not to say that competitive procurements do not occur, but rather that the details of many contracts are obtained through well-established relationships with state or local officials. State or municipal entities use simplified versions of the federal RFP, including a request for letter bids or qualification packages similar to large private-sector clients.

Every federal proposal-whether large or small, sole source or competitive, fixed price or cost plus fixed fee-requires a statement of the need, background, and hoped-for results in using consulting services. At times, a financial analysis of the benefits versus the costs of obtaining them is done. State agencies are also aware of this procedure, but few have the statutory mandate to require a needs justification. Municipal consulting contracts rarely have an official justification. (Where an RFP is used, federal or state agencies select consultants by committee and client approval) At the municipal level, proposals are circulated to government officials and noncompeting outside experts for evaluation. Based on these comments, awards are made by officials.

The federal government has preassigned conditions for any contract and a standard procedure for determining what the payment scheme should be. Again, the state and municipal contract terms are more variable.

Contract costs between state agencies and professional consultants are reached in one of three ways:

1. By negotiations between the consultant and the contracting agency representative,
2. By the agency's acceptance of the consultant's proposal outlining the cost of the services to be rendered, or
3. By agency policy that establishes fair compensation to the consultant.

Other contract terms are determined through negotiations between the consultant and the agency representative. Few states have a standard contract form; fewer municipalities have one. Most contractual agreements for consulting services are drawn up after the decision to retain an consultant is made, not before as at the federal level.

Procedures for monitoring the consulting work are generally established, at least in principle, at all levels of government. Procedures are defined for periodic progress reports, modifications to work effort, and minor contractual changes. However, in practice the federal government enforces these policies the most, the states to some degree, and the municipalities barely at all. By contrast, no level of government has well established methods for evaluating the consultant's effort and relating this effort to the initial justification. However, in practice, all levels have tried to evaluate the results of the consulting services provided. The least amount of control exists in implementing the consultant's recommendations. This statement is true at any government level, and the reasons are many:

- Obligations end when the contract runs out.
- No provisions for implementing recommendations in contract.
- Frenetic changes in programs and agency personnel tend to deemphasize consulting results.
- Lack of measuring tools for consulting work.
- Inability to have procurement follow through to ensure that benefits will exceed costs.
- Lack of line and staff officials support for contract and results.

Sample Task V

Given the differences in procuring contracts among federal, state, and local agencies, would you change your marketing approach in expanding your clients from federal to state or local? Why? If yes, what changes would be made?

Case Example 10-1: Expansion High, or Explosion Blues?

Infi-Del, Inc. has had a terrific year. As a provider of acoustical consulting to new cable franchises, its reputation has become known throughout the Southeast. In fact, the majority of the firm's work has been obtained through word of mouth. For the past three years the two owners have met with the cable franchises, outlined the scope of what they can do, and entered into a handshake agreement to provide the specific services. The audio design work they do is of high quality, yet it requires putting in long hours over a short period.

Not long ago, the State of Florida issued a solicitation for a two-year contract to modernize and upgrade its teleconferencing capability. The scope of work included a feasibility study, demonstration and testing of technical improvements, and the implementation of an expanded teleconferencing capability.

One owner of Infi-Del, Judy Skeptic, read an article about this solicitation in a trade magazine. She discussed the project with her co-owner, Jim Refit, and they decided to answer the proposal. After obtaining a copy of the proposal request, they felt even more confident about their ability to perform the work. Also, this contract would give them a longer-term, steadier stream of income. So bid they did, following the instructions listed therein.

About a month later, Judy received a call from the State Communication Office. The caller, Mr. Ed Justify, asked Judy right away whether she had ever submitted a proposal to the State of Florida. "It appears you have at best a crude understanding of how to present your ideas," Justify stated bluntly. "In fact, if I had not heard of you from a friend who owns a cable franchise, I would not have even called." He went on to say that the substance of Judy's and Jim's proposal had little justification or perspective. It is like a "snake-oil sales pitch." Further, Justify said that their management plan was simply to do the work and collect a paycheck afterward.

"That's simply not how things are done," he added. He suggested that they withdraw and resubmit a subcontract proposal to the winning bidder. "You mean we will have to work for someone else in order to work for you?," Skeptic asked. "You got it," Justify answered.

The contract award was announced about a month later.

Skeptic and Refit talked with the winner, a prominent communications conglomerate, CCG, and the two parties agreed to a subcontract arrangement. Quickly, Skeptic and Refit put a proposal together. Within a week they were working on the teleconferencing contract.

Two months later, Ed Justify gave Judy a call. "Remember me, your source of funds? I thought I'd call to say that you're in real trouble. Judy, I spoke with my cable contact, who said you were doing some private consulting for him. Did you also know that CCG is in the cable business? Working for two competitors concurrently without their mutual consent is a conflict of interest and grounds for immediate termination." Judy began, "We had no idea ...." Ed interrupted, "I assumed this, as you appear to know little about contracting. So you have a choice. Since you are working for our mutual friend now, either sign a statement saying you will not work for him at the same time as for any cable company in the same service area, or stop work immediately on this contract." Judy retorted, "Working for someone else besides myself is just the pits."

SUMMARY AND EXTENSION

Federal consulting is changing, with new regulations, cutbacks, and contracting officers who generally complicate the procurement process and increase the time it takes to award a contract. In addition, the competition for consulting work is increasing. This chapter has shown how techniques and insights can be used to overcome the contracting constraints. Yet there are some observations worth noting:

- Procurement is a personal and procedural activity. Knowing the process is fine, but getting to know the contracting official is as important as, if not more important than, doing a consulting assignment.
- Background investigation is critical. If you would like to perform, let's say, strategic planning for the Department of Energy, see who you know and find out the potential interest.
- The more variables there are, the more things there are that can go wrong.

Recognize this at the outset in seeking government consulting. Take steps to stay on top of the process and form contingencies for unexpected situations.

- Realize that federal consulting has a legacy such that you will be as much a participant as an observer, a teacher as a learner, and a giver as a receiver. (This statement is also true for foreign consulting, as shown in the next chapter.)

In Chapter Eleven, the insights gathered here and the observations above are further applied to consulting in a different culture. The success of any foreign assignment depends on the ability to couch the engagement in terms and actions readily understandable by the client.

Chapter Eleven

Consulting Abroad

When a consultant from one country undertakes an assignment in another, distinct cultural differences must be dealt with. These differences can hinder or help your performance. To increase the likelihood of the latter, the consultant must prepare even more extensively for a foreign assignment than with domestic consulting. A suggested modus operandi is shown in Exhibit 11-1. Before putting this exhibit into use, the consultant must learn about the client's culture, as outlined in Exhibit 11-2. Exhibit 11-3 provides the ways to achieve cultural orientation, and Exhibit 11-4 shows you how to use cultural information in preparing to intervene. In addition, the consultant can discover which cultural factors assist or hamper meeting a foreign client's objectives. As Exhibit 11-5 shows, such efforts can be recognized and dealt with as the assignment progresses. The consulting process in a foreign country is similar to the one described in Chapter Six.

But there are some differences, which are listed in Exhibit 11-6. Three underlying assumptions to any successful foreign consulting engagement are:

- The client will consider adopting changes to the extent that they are presented in the cultural framework of the client organization.
- The client will accept the consulting activity if client confidence is: first, secured for the consultant's presence; second, sustained for the program of change; third, affirmed for the consulting process; fourth, reinforced for each step in the process; and fifth, used to evaluate the effort and then increased in future dealings with the issue without the consultant's assistance.
- Training is required as the primary medium to build and carry through the client/consultant relationship.

EXHIBIT 11-1

Modus Operandi for Foreign Consulting

Acute understanding about assignment

↓

Insights about client culture

↓

Insights about client and his organization

↓

Methods for relating information

↓

Assignment defined in client culture terms

↓

Assignment done by preserving client culture

↓

Client acceptance of outcome is through jointly approved effort

↓

Client participates in outcome through training

EXHIBIT 11-2

Accept of Client Culture and Consultant Culture

Attribute	Description	Client Culture	Consultant Culture Response	Comments
Lnaguage	Spoken language Dialect Nonverbal cues Organizational terminology, codes, or slang			
Appearance	Customs, regulations, and variations by job type by geographic area			

Conduct of business	Method of making contact Method of negotiating Rapport established
Socializing	Preparation and types of food eaten When, where, and how social interaction occurs in the organization
Sense of time	Degree of importance Timekeeping customs Working hours flexibility
Relationships	Due to Age Sex Status Power Wisdom Family ties Types of personal interactions
Values	Implicit, informal norms of behavior Attitudes about work, career, society, change, politics, health, etc. Beliefs about consultants
Learning	Kind of reasoning Emphasis on learning Response to change

EXHIBIT 11-3

Steps to Consultant's Foreign Assignment

Step	*Elements*	*Approximate Time Period*	*Resources*
Preparation		2–6 months	1. American Management Association, 135 W. 50th St., New York, NY 10020; Contact: John C. Cunningham; Subject: How to Do Business in . .
			2. Intercultural Network, Inc., 906 N. Spring Ave., La Grange Park, IL 60525; Contact: David S. Hoopes; Subject: Intercultural Training
	Selection for assignment	1 month	1. American Graduate School of International Management, Thunderbird Campus, Glendale, AZ 85306; Contact: R. Duane Hall; Subject: International Management Training
			2. A. R. Lanier, "Selecting and Preparing Personnel for Overseas Transfer," *Personnel Journal*, Vol. 58, No. 3, 1979, pp. 160-163
	Language training	2 months	1. Berlitz Publications, Inc., Ridgefield, NJ 07657; Subject: Self-Teaching Courses

		2. The World Trade Institute, One World Trade Center, 55th Floor, New York, NY 10047; Contact: Peter C. Goldmark, Jr.; Subject: Language School
International business training	1 month	1. The World Trade Institute (as above)
		2. The Business Council for International Understanding, The American University, Washington, DC 20016; Contact: Gary E. Lloyd; Subject: How to Do Business
		3. Nancy E. Briggs and Glenn R. Harwood, "Training Personnel in Multinational Business: An Inoculation Approach," *International Journal of Intercultural Relations*, Vol. 6, No. 4, 1982, pp. 341–354
Intercultural discussions, training, and practice	1 month	1. Overseas Briefing Associates, 201 East 36th St., New York, NY 10016; Contact: Alison R. Lanier; Subject: Training and Briefing for Consultants and Families
		2. Intercultural Network, Inc. (as above)

			3. Pierre Casse, *Training for the Cross- Cultural Mind* (Washington, D.C.: Society for Intercultural Education, 1979)
	Logistics, departure, and travel	1 month	1. Intercultural Communications, Inc., P.O. Box 14358, University Station, Minneapolis, MN 55414; Contact: Helen L. McNulty; Subject: Relocation and Departure Training
			2. Eleanor R. Pierce, *All You Need to Know About Living Abroad* (Garden City, NY: Doubleday & Co., 1980)
Entry	On-site orientation	1 week to 1 month	Center for Research and Education, 1800 Pontiac, Denver, CO 80220; Contact: Albert R. Wright; Subject: Cross-Cultural Orientation
	Culture shock	1–3 months	L. Robert Kohls, *Survival Kit for Overseas Living* (Chicago: Intercultural Network, 1979)
	Acclimation to client organization	2–3 months	Fred Rosenweig et al., "Water and Sanitation for Health Project," Camp Dresser and McKee, Arlington, VA, 1983.

Integration	Accultura-tion to host culture	1/2–4 months	1. P. Benson, "Measuring Cross-Culture Adjust-ment: The Problem of Criteria," *International Journal of Intercultural Relations,* Vol. 2, No. 1, 1978, pp. 2137
	Evolution of life-style	2–6 months	2. Benjamin J. Broome, "Facilitating Attitudes and Message Character-istics in the Expression of Differences in Inter-cultural Encounters," *International Journal of Intercultural Relations,* Vol. 5, No. 3, 1981, pp. 215–237
Assign-ment execution	Joint effort Client able to handle similar future prob-lems with-out aid of consultant Completion occurs with-out disrupt-ing cultural attributes	2 months–2 years	1. Dennis A. Rondinelli, "Why Development Projects Fail," *Project Management Quarterly,* Vol. VII, No. 2, March 1976
			2. American Society for Personnel Administra-tion, 30 Park Drive, Berea, OH 44107, (216)826-4790; Subject: International Personnel Management Seminars
			3. Coverdale Organization, *Managing Effectively Across Cultures,* London and Washington, DC

Exit preparation	Withdrawal	1–3 months	James A. Burruss, "Cross-Cultural Transfer of Competency-Based Technologies," McBer and Company, Boston, MA, 1983.
	Logistics and travel	1 month	
Reentry	Reentry shock	*1/2–2* months	1. Intercultural Communication, Inc., P.O. Box 14358, University Station, Minneapolis, MN 44414; Contact: Helen L. McNulty; Subject: Reentry Training
			2. Vincent A. Miller, *The Guidebook for International Trainers* (New York: Von Nostrand,1979), Chap. 3
	Reorientation to work environment	1–4 months	Emmett Wallace, "Conducting Management Training Overseas," Educational Systems and Designs, Inc., Westport, CT, 1983
Reintegration	Life-style readjustment	2–8 months	1. American Society for Personnel Administration, 30 Park Drive, Berea, OH 44107; (216)8264790; International Personnel Management Seminars
	Assignment follow-up and future work	3–6 months	2. U.S.A.I.D,, Foreign Service Institute, Washington, DC; Community Action Seminars

EXHIBIT 11-4

Example of Using Exhibit 11 : Consulting

Attribute	Client-Culture	Consultant Culture Response	Comments
Language	Learns English or uses an interpreter	Required to have a guide who can serve as interpreter as needed	
	Distance between two communicators is greater than in the West	Is direct, formal dialogue without much nonverbal use	
	Organizational terminology is specific to job or production functions.	Discussion using slang, gestures, political references, or jokes is inappropriate.	
Appearance	Is very clean, neat, well groomed and polished across all strata of society.	Dress is different from most Chinese, but always be neat.	Do not imitate Chinese style of dress.
Conduct of business	Prefer personal contact. Negotiations occur after cultural barriers are bridged and formal rapport in place. Temperament is subdued and with respect	Seek client entry in person as *prefer* able to letter or telephone contact. Be prepared for long negotiations in which cultural sensitivity is demonstrated. Contract is achieved only with mutual respect and understanding.	
Socializing	Family name is always mentioned first.	If host name is Teng Hsiao-Ping, should be addressed Mr. Teng.	

	Host invites visitors first. Offers tea and cigarettes. Expects change of pleasantries, precise discussion of topic at its current stage, and states when meeting is over.	Come prepared to negotiate/ communicate in formal, logical, and systematic manner. Also have future negotiations in place of your choosing.	
	Host will hold frequent banquets.	As the honored guest, arrive early, return toasts, be the first to depart after the meal is finished, and reciprocate.	
Sense of time	Very important. Host is punctual and expects others to be. Meeting times are set before hand and are regular. Length of meeting is short.	Follow host's example.	Give formal apologies if tardiness or post ponement occurs.
Relationships	China prides itself on degree of urban/ rural, man/woman, and laborer/owner equality. Family is important but family ties are second to economic ties.	For foreigners the emphasis differs. Give equal courtesy to all Chinese. Give verbal complements and, where appropriate, gifts from United States. But, do not tip.	
	Communication begins with bow and brief shake of hands.	Follow this custom. Do not be loud, rude, overly aggressive,	

	Group is focus of interaction, not individual. Certain types of behavior are not tolerated.	or judgmental in conversations and exchange.
Values	Hosts are industrious, hardworking, committed to industrial progress, political service, and social betterment. Change comes deliberately but slowly.	Show dignity, reserve, patience, persistence, and sensitivity to and respect for customs and temperament.
Learning	Most Chinese are educated to know a trade or skill, to give service to society, and to have a thorough cultural grounding. Learning is rapid in technical areas, less so in behavioral areas.	Modus operandi is to consult in technical matters first, then to follow up with behavioral or training concerns.

Adapted in part from Philip R. Harris and Robert T. Moran, *Managing Cultural Differences* (Houston: Gulf Publishing Co., 1979), Chapter 18.

Usually, the consulting engagement is carried out as a three-way effort among the consultant, client, and a funding agency.

Generally, the agency first recognizes the need for consulting assistance and selects the consultant. Making agency contact and submitting proposals to various development institutions is a common way of securing foreign assignments.

Alternatively, working for foreign governments or firms through association contacts or referrals is plausible (see the Addendum).

Sample Task I

How would being an international consultant alter the operations of your business? Are foreign assignments better handled by firms, or individuals? Why?

EXHIBIT 11-5

Synthesis of Client and Consultant Cultures—for Chinese Experience

Expediting Factors to Assignment	*Means of Using Throughout Assignment*	*Inhibiting Factors to Assignment*	*Means of Elimininating*	*Comments*
Series of meetings	Effective scheduling	Not knowing when client disapproves	Get to know client group better	
			Find appropriate occasion to discuss this with client	
Consistency	In dress and meeting style	Failure to reciprocate socially	Formal apology done orally (with written copy) before client group	

EXHIBIT 11-6

Differences in Domestic and Foreign Consulting

Consulting Process Step	*Domestic Mode*	*Foreign Mode*
Awareness of the issue	Client governs awareness and decision to use consultant.	External party recognizes need for consultant.
Finding the right consultant	Client and client group interview, evaluate, and choose consultant.	Funding agency selects consultant for client. Consultant prepares to work in different culture.

Starting the assignment	Client and consultant meet to develop rapport.	Consultant overcomes culture shock with client assistance if needed. Cultural attributes form basis for rapport.
Defining the issue	Consultant forms impression of issue and reaches consensus with client.	Issue understanding reached through specific cultural practices.
Means to resolve issue	Alternatives are developed and presented to client for discussion and client decision.	Alternatives are presented with full awareness of the cultural implications. Client is the final decision maker.
Implementing the chosen alternative	Consultant implements and monitors changes as well as works through resistances and conflicts.	Consultant trains client and staff in how to implement and subsequently use resolutions to issue. Effort is exerted to increase client acceptance of changes couched in terms of the client's cultural milieu.
Termination and evaluation	Client and consultant examine impacts and implications of assignment. Follow-up arrangements are ascertained.	Client critiques the consulting assignment. Influence of assignment on local economy and local consulting is discussed. Further, future client/consultant and agency contact is determined.

Sample Task II

Comment on the following: When consulting abroad, the consultant is put into an ambassador position. That is, he or she must perform the work in a professional manner without violating the laws, regulations, or values of the host country. Any infringement of professional standards could have repercussions for the consultant's government.

Name	Address	Director	Founding Date	Membership	Description of Activities	Publications
International Association of Consulting Actuaries (IACA)	600 Third Ave. New York, NY 10016	Evan Innes	1968	374	Aim is to facilitate contact between consulting actuaries on an international basis. IACA arranges meetings to fulfill this objective. Members in 18 countries.	
International Marketing Public Relations and Advertising Consultants (IMPA)	c/o Yellow Hammer Co. Ltd. 3 Wellington Square London SW 3 Tele: (441)730-8294		1975		Purpose of IMPA is to group similar association from European countries	
International Association of Economics Consultants	BP 7135 Amsterdam 1009,	Stephanus de Jong				

Organization	Address	Contact	Founded	Members	Purpose	Publications
International Federation of Consulting Engineers (FIDIC)	Netherlands 206 Groot Hertoginnenlaan P.O. Box 17334 2502 CH Den Haag, Netherlands Tele: (3120)604828	A. H. Campbell	1913	32	Members are national associations in 32 countries. Purposes of FIDIC are to promote and protect interests of association, encourage formulating and using standards of conduct, and facilitate cooperation with other organizations involved in technical work. Has developed model agreements between client and consultant engineer.	Conditions of Contract Client/Consultant Rules of Agreement Interview International Model Form of Agreement
European Community of Consulting Engineers	11 Rue de la Neva F-75008 Paris, France		1977			

Name	Address	Director	Founding Date	Membership	Description of Activities	Publications
International Confederation of Associations of Exports and Consultants (Appraisers) (CIDADEC)	Siege Admn. Rue Ten Bosch 85 Bte 85 B-1050 Brussels, Belgium	Jean G. Bastin	1953	72,000	Members are national associations representing 25 countries. Aims are to coordinate the fundamental principles of the appraising profession, and to codify the legal provisions concerning the profession. Holds annual meetings.	Index of Categories and Specialists of Experts and Consultants International Registry of Consultants
International Consultants Foundation (ICF)	5605 Lamar Rd. Washington, DC 20016 (301)320-4409	Gordon Lippitt			ICF founded to harness resources of consultants involved in international	CF International Consulting News International Consultant Registry

European Committee of Industrial Consultants Services	c/o Instit Econo mique et Social des Classes Moyennes Rue de Congres 33 B-1000 Brussels, Belgium Tele: (322)21934-39	Willy Degryse	1969	change. Goal is to effectively implement change strategies in international organizations and develop- ing countries. ICF carries out registration program, client referral service, and annual conferences.

Name	Address	Director	Founding Date	Membership	Description of Activities	Publications
European Federation of Management Consultants' Associations (FEACO)	c/o Syntec 3 Rue Leon Bonnat F-75016 Paris, France Tele: (331)52444353	Emile Laboureau	1960	15	Members are national associations representing 15 countries. Aims of FEACO are to promote and protect the mutual professional interest of member organizations, to encourage the setting up of standards for professional conduct, and to encourage formation of such associations in countries which do not have them. Has an annual congress of members.	

Organization	Address	Contact	Year	Number	Description
International Association of Political Consultants (IAPC)	One Dag Hammarskjold Plaza Suite 1819 New York, NY 10019 (212)421-8984	F. Clifton White	1968	60	IAPC provides a forum for the exchange of ideas and techniques on politics, campaigning, and government relations. Members are individuals engaged fulltime in such activities. AAPC is the U.S. branch of IAPC.
International Society of Consultants on Synthesis	20 Rue Lafitte F-75009 Paris, France Tele: (331)7709144				An enterprise functioning as a management consultancy whose members are affiliated with the Federation for the Respect of Man and Humanity and related organizations.

Name	*Address*	*Director*	*Found-ing Date*	*Membership*	*Description of Activities*	*Publications*
World Council of Manage-ment (CI OS)	c/o Nederlandse Vereniging Voor Manage-ment Van Alkemadelaan 700 Den Haag 2019, Nether-lands Tele: (3170)264331	8. Bouwens	1926	36	Members are national orga-nizations rep-resenting 363 countries. CIOS coordinates efforts of mem-ber organiza-tions and holds assembly every 3 years.	CIOS Manual
International Federation of Operational Research Soci-eties (IFORS)	c/o IMSOR Bldg. 349 DK-2800 Lyngby, Den-mark Tele: (452)884433	Ms. Helle Welling	1959	31	Members are national organizations representing 31 countries. Specialized meetings and conferences held annually to further opera-tional research.	IFORS Bulletin International Abstracts in Operations Research

European Association for Personnel Management (EAPM)	Director Deutsche Gesellschaft fur Personalfuhrung Kaiserswerther Strasse 137 D-4000 Dusseldorf, 30, West Germany	Hans Friedrichs	1962	14	Members are national associations representing 14 countries. EAPM's function is to promote use of and professional standards for personnel management.
Asian Associations of Personnel Management (AAPM)	c/o Bengal Chamber of Commerce and Industry 23 An Mookerjee Rd. Calcutta 700001, India Tele: (0)232951		1968	5	Members are national associations from India, Philippines, Sri Lanka, Thailand, and Australia. AAPM wishes to form member organizations in countries where they do not exist, as

Name	Address	Director	Founding Date	Membership	Description of Activities	Publications
					well as act as clearinghouse for exchange of ideas and research findings. Also, AAPM encourages liason with similar organizations.	
Consultative Group of Actuaries of Countries of the European Communities	Staple Inn Hall High Holborn London WCIV 725, England Tele: (441)2420106 WILPF	John M. Henty	1978	9	Members are national organizations in 9 countries.	
Conference of Non Governmental Organizations in Consultative	1 Rue de Varembe CH-1211	Ms. Edith Ballantyne	1950	20	Members are all nongovernmental organizations (NGO) enjoying consul	

Status with the United Nations Economic and Social Council (CONGO)	Geneva 20, Switzerland Tele: (4122)336175				tative status. Purpose is to promote opportunities for NGOs to provide services, exchange views, and further effectiveness of U.N. programs.	
European Committee of the Consulting Engineers of the Common Market (CEDIC)	Hotel Ravenstein 3 Rue Ravenstei B-1000 Brussels, Belgium Tele: (322)511-S2-94	S. D'Hoore	1965	10	Members are national associations of consulting engineers.ç	Conference Report International Agreements

Name	Address	Director	Founding Date	Membership	Description of Activities	Publications
European Committee of Consulting Engineers	Bol.de Water-loo 103 B-1000 Brussels, Belgium		1971		Professional organization representing engineers within the European Economic Community countries.	
Latin American Federation of Consulting Engineers	Av. R Rivera Navarrette 451 Piso 3 OF 313 Lima 27, Peru Tele: (5114)404706	Manuel A. Villaran	1972	10	Members are national associations in Latin American countries.	

SUMMARY AND EXTENSION

Chapters Ten and Eleven have extended the consultant's engagements to include public-sector and foreign clients. The major differences from the private sector in performing consulting for these clients are the number of client representatives, the nature of the contractual relationship, and the complexity of the engagement. If demand for your consulting services becomes large and complex and thus requires delegating some consulting effort, you might consider hiring others to meet the growing client requests. The next chapter deals with whether or not to form a large organization. The answer depends on how you view your future development and involvement.

ADDENDUM: DIGEST OF FOREIGN CONSULTING ASSOCIATIONS UPDATE

In the format of Chapter Nine, a partial list of European, Asian, and Latin American consulting organizations and American organizations, with foreign emphasis is given on the following pages. The information shows organization, address, phone, head of organization, founding date, number of members, description of activities, and publications.[1] Further, most European, British Commonwealth, Latin American, and Asian countries have their own engineering consultant societies and business consulting associations.

---

[1]Union of International Associations, *Yearbook of International Organizations,* 19th ed., Union of International Associations, Brussels, Belgium, 1981.

Chapter Twelve

Expanding Your Consulting Practice

SNAPSHOT

At this point we have examined all the elements of an independent consultancy and how they are applied to various potential clients. But how do you discover whether it is best for your business and your desires to form a formal organization to support your consulting services? This chapter explores this notion with the following assumptions:

- Managing a firm is not for everyone.
- Successfully operating a firm requires emphasizing employees' personal needs and career development.
- Planning is essential; without it, the firm's success is in jeopardy.
- The long-term viability of the enterprise depends on incorporating the lessons learned from client engagements.

Besides' the traditional management activities (planning, organizing, staffing, and controlling), a section is presented on how to diversify or sell the business. The chapter's objective is to give you the opportunity to assess whether managing people and resources together with client engagements is for you.

FORMING A FIRM

Thus far, we have focused on the solo practitioner. Although forming a firm is usually a way to earn more money and to distribute consulting services to a larger audience, it is not for everyone. Exhibit 12-1 explores when it is time to consider enlarging a consulting practice.

EXHIBIT 12-1

To Expand into a Firm?

Pro	*Con*	*Comments*
Increase in sales revenue	Manage larger overhead	
Increase in profits	Shift effort from consulting to marketing and administrative activities	
Increase image and influence	Change emphasis and preference of consulting work	
Form an organization	Unable to retain individual operations and work style	
Manage people	Devote significant effort to staffing and evaluating employees	
Innovate new services	Improve reputation	
Capture market segment	Larger concern with competition	

Sample Task 1

Complete Exhibit 12-1 and see if a pattern emerges. Are you not ready to open a firm now, but willing to consider one in the near future? Do you prefer a loose teaming arrangement? Or do you want to remain an independent consultant?

Repeat this exercise after you have completed reading this chapter.

Have your perceptions changed? Why?

CHANGING OWNERSHIP

If you decide to develop a consulting firm, you must first ask yourself:

Which legal and tax structure will suit my objectives? Since single or multiple owners assume full responsibility for all losses, and since employing additional personnel entails additional capital, incorporating may be best because the liabilities are borne by the business, not the individual. According to the U.S. Census Bureau, the majority of consulting establishments become corporations when they acquire employees. (The steps in incorporating are described in Chapter Three.) Yet bear in mind that you need ample funds and abilities to operate a firm. A mismatch between capital and know-how, or number of employees and contracts, will cause instabilities leading to poor management, performance, and reputation. Grow as your money supply expands and abilities increase, but no faster.

If a project calls for additional money or skills, short-term options are available to you. As a corporation, you can secure a short-term loan for the project at hand and charge the interest as part of administration costs (as illustrated in Chapter Eight). To obtain additional professional staff, you can subcontract with another firm that would receive a set percentage of the client contract dollars in return for supplying the labor required for the assignment. You can also use temporary services for administrative clerical staff as the need arises. Permanent staff should be added only when all other avenues have been exhausted. Now, many firms do not follow this modus operandi, but it is one way to achieve and maintain stable growth.

ORGANIZING A FIRM

Unlike the statistics for ownership, there are no data on the types of organizations consultants create. However, it can be surmised that most firms operate in one of the three standard organizational forms:

Functional. There are units for each major facet of operation: administration, personnel, marketing, and financial control. Authority is generally centralized. Career paths are directed upward to higher management levels.

Service. There are units for special service areas: survey analysis, economic modeling, transportation system design, employee compensation, energy conservation, and product evaluation. And for all service areas there are centralized support functions personnel, report production, administration, and accounting. Authority is delegated to the head of each service area and to the functional managers. Career paths are broader but still with an "up or out" philosophy.

Matrix. There are units for service areas linked with current projects and functional areas such as biology, physics, or mathematics. Employees report to a functional head, but work primarily with project managers. Basic departments-administration and financial control-are either self contained within each functional area or centralized. Authority is widely dispersed. Career paths are lateral or horizontal.

A consulting firm's major output is articulated expertise; its major input is people. Consequently, a consulting firm must be more flexible, creative, and sensitive to the needs of its members. It must be able to respond to-if not anticipate--changes in its environment. One way to achieve this is through adopting a design. The design establishes how business is done, how decisions are made, and how members gain experience and responsibilities. There are steps in designing an organization.

First, recognize that external or internal events create pressure to change operations. Second, fulfill subsequent consulting engagements. Third, increase the effectiveness of operations. Fourth, expand variety and intensity of services offered. Fifth, reorganize to reflect changes in firm environment brought about by first four steps. Further, this design method works for any organizational form.

This sequence of events does not just happen; in fact, it will never occur in the majority of consulting firms because members become rigid and fail to respond to change. This problem can be handled at the outset by balancing the why and what of the organization's design. This can be achieved by acknowledging that each professional member of the firm whether an entry-level consultant or an owner-can perform various tasks.

How is a design put in place? The firm owners or directors, senior and junior consultants, form a group to discuss professional, technical, administrative, and at times, personal concerns. This "org-group" is the catalyst for innovation and the channel for change.

FORMULATING POLICIES AND PLANS

Once the organization design is in place, firm policies must be formulated. In succinct terms, a policy is a guideline for decision making. A procedure consists of the operational steps required to carry out a policy. Both reflect the firm's thinking and both are receptive to dange. Exhibit 12-2 presents an example of personnel policy. For example, C1 and C2, professional and support positions, are policy statements of the staff positions which govern decisions about the firm's staffing goals. Yet C3 and C4, hiring and evaluation procedures, are the concrete ways in which these policy statements are implemented. Exhibit 12-3 is an example of a consulting firm's personnel policies. A policy **is** usually promulgated through a formal communication channel-a memo that informs all staff of changes in procedure. Such information can also be passed along at a firmwide meeting, principal and staff working groups, or at individual evaluations.

However the message is communicated, keep in mind the following: Is the data transmittal necessary, and if so, is it being communicated in the most receptive manner?

EXHIBIT 12-2

Personnel Policy Manual

Table of Contents

A. Introduction

B. General Company Information
1. History
2. Purpose and Goals
3. Services Provided
4. Operating Philosophy

C. Staff Functions
1. Professional Positions
2. Support Positions
3. Hiring Practices
4. Evaluation Procedures
5. Advancement
6. Ethics
7. Termination
8. Communications/Public Relations

D. Employee Benefits
1. Salary Levels
2. Overtime Pay
3. Wages and Taxes
4. Vacations, Sick Leave, and Holidays
5. Compensation Time and Absences
6. Injury or Illness
7. Insurance
8. Bonus Plan
9. Profit Sharing
10. Retirement Plan
11. Credit Union

E. Office Operations
1. New Employees
2. Hours of Work
3. Pay Procedures
4. Mail
5. Use of Office Space
6. Parking
7. Purchasing Requirements
8. Solicitations or Visitors to Office
9. Keys
10. Energy Conservation
11. Use of Telephone, Photocopier, and Other Office Equipment
12. Patents/Inventions
13. Filing
14. Cutting Overhead Costs
15. Safety and Health Precautions
16. Business Expense Forms

F. Career Development
1. In-House Training
2. External Training
3. Professional Activities/ Memberships

EXHIBIT 12-3

Concerns Relating to Firm Members

Preamble: Syner-Think, Inc., was founded to espouse a professionally competitive firm within the consulting service marketplace. To this end, we, the firm, believe that people are the most valuable firm resource. To discover, harness, and further the value of the firm members, certain conditions must be met. The firm:

- Must develop a stimulating work environment;
- Must create and sustain opportunities for advancement through monetary, intellectual, and leadership incentives;
- Must be receptive to and incorporate, where possible, suggested changes to the firm environment, work procedures, interpersonal interactions, and client/consultant relations;
- Must strive to reinforce commitments to keep personnel concerns a high priority.

Guidelines: The statements listed below represent Syner-Think's personnel positions. These positions depict the expectations and compensations for work effort expended. But, as with all serious endeavors, they alone are necessary but not sufficient. Effective procedures are the means to achieve these policies.

- Any professional staff member is compensated for consulting endeavors by salary, a benefits package, and bonus and fringe rewards.
- Salaries will be competitive with other consulting firms. The total monetary compensation includes benefits and bonus inducements and tends to be higher than that of most firms.
- The benefits package consists of health and life insurance, vacation, holiday and sick leave, credit union privileges, retirement plans, and reimbursement for education.
- Bonus and fringe benefits include merit income awards, additional "comp" time, profit-sharing, stock options, and gifts for creative contributions.
- Syner-Think is to have definite career paths that are to be tested as the firm expands.
- The growth of the firm is tied to the degree of upward mobility. The firm seeks lucrative consulting contracts using dollar skills and career development criteria.

- Employee selection, acclimation, performance evaluation, and advancement is done carefully and to foster mutual and growing enthusiasm and satisfaction among firm members and between management and staff,
- We seek to maintain a well-balanced group of professional consultants in terms of age, experience, maturity, communication potential, and abilities.

Once policies and procedures are known, the firm's activities must be presented in a systematic manner to provide consulting successfully now and in the future. For example, a marketing plan can show a coherent, consistent approach to achieving marketing objectives. However, accomplishing marketing objectives is uncertain. The uncertainty is lessened only as more and more of the plan is realized. But by then it is time to modify the plan. Thus Exhibit 12-4 presents a sample of the primary elements in a marketing plan. The plan, in essence, describes the firm's previous efforts, the failings of these efforts, future directions, and how they will be carried out. The plan's heart is it s objectives:

Feasibility. Do the objectives make sense? Can they be carried out with existing resources? Will they obtain the hoped-for results?

EXHIBIT 12-4

Major Components of a Marketing Plan

Component	*Description*
Preamble	Summary
	Note general relationships to firm
Prior marketing activities	Past marketing efforts
	Past marketing constraints
	Past market trends
Current market	Description of current market forces
	Present opportunities
Objectives	Achievements for this time period
	(year) Relationship to overall
	corporate goals
Strategies	Means of accomplishing objectives
	Resources required
	Policies and procedures necessitated
Constraints	Objective constraints Strategy
	constraints Ways to overcome them

Consistency. Is each objective related to another one? Are all objectives related to general corporate goals? Are any objectives in conflict?

Measurability. Can tangible results be compared to past trends? Can the results be used to formulate plans?

Operational. How soon can each objective be realized? Are the objectives based on present firm resources? What are their positive features? What are their disadvantages? Strategies show how the firm will achieve growth by meeting its objectives. In general, there is a separate strategy for each objective, although two or more objectives could be met by one strategy. The strategy tests the *objectives* by determining if resources, wherewithal, and abilities exist to go after the defined market area and to do so in a cost-effective way.

The strategy is also designed to assess whether any long-range activities are possible. The strategy also tests a portion of the market first before moving on to wider coverage. Finally, the thrust of strategy development is to use a minimal number of strategies to accomplish all objectives.

Exhibit 12-5 illustrates a marketing plan. After a plan is developed, it is reviewed for completeness and realism. Throughout the year, periodic

---

EXHIBIT 12-5

Sample Marketing Plan for a Consulting Firm

Marketing 1983: A Choice for All Seasons

Prelude: This year proves to be a crossroads. For the past three years, our marketing efforts have caused us, more or less, to flounder and juggle our activities. With a new managing director and the recent success of our financial service line, marketing in 1983 will be better planned, coordinated, and executed than in any time since the founding of the firm.

Previous Marketing: Our initial attempts to sell insulation were product-oriented. The failure of our production schedules taught us a valuable lesson—stay in tune with customer thinking and service scheduling. Last year's marketing plan was our first try at balancing these two. We targeted a modest 15 percent increase in client billings while trying to more than double our billable time. Also, we tended to concentrate new sales in our immediate geographic locale. The results have been mixed. A large third-quarter contract caused our charge time to exceed our expectations. But the number of new clients fell short of our projections. Possibly, the decrease in hours spent on marketing by senior staff explains our lack of new clients.

Current Market Situation: In the last nine months the economy has worsened, but demand for our services has grown. Competitors have also shown increased billings, and since our client market tends to be new users of these services, the year's activity could be profitable. In addition, we are getting referrals in sufficient quantity to sustain us even if new client areas do not materialize.

Objectives for 1983: We want to accomplish:
- 20 percent increase in sales
- 40 percent increase in new clients
- Sales in two new market areas
- Development of at least two new services and subservices
- Effective use of television advertising

Strategies to meet the objectives:
- Emphasize small-order contracts
- Push for repeat business from large accounts
- Expand our geographic coverage
- Develop policies that allow all professional staff to participate in the marketing effort
- Establish service teams to upgrade service quality and provision
- Advertise to individual clients
- Budget for a television commercial for a local audience
- Establish marketing team to find new contracts, locales, and markets with tests done on all three

Constraints: Unlike last year, when we didn't "chew" enough, our "bite" may be too large this year. Training and communication with all staff in carrying out the strategies is of utmost importance. The time and energy devoted to business development will probably increase our administrative charges 12 percent on contract billings. But the firmwide push will produce such intangible benefits as increased morale, productivity, and results. These, in turn, could yield tangible revenues as early as the third quarter. Each of us needs the other's effort if together we are to make broader inroads in our large potential market.

meetings are held to update the plan, incorporate lessons from client engagement, eliminate unrealistic objectives, and test new strategies. In similar fashion, a financial, human resources, and corporate plan can be developed and, together with the marketing plan, integrated and implemented.

DECIDING TO STAFF

People who operate one-person firms tend to be highly motivated and independent. They also tend to view their responsibility toward a client as self -centered. That is, to ensure the best service, the consultant completes the project alone. This attitude often produces remarkable results, yet it makes it difficult to hire additional staff.

Exhibit 12-6 explores some of the key factors to consider in staffing. The basic concerns are when, how many employees, why, and under what

---

EXHIBIT 12-6

Decision Quandary

To Staff or Not to Staff—Is This the Right Question?

Factor	*Pro*	*Con*	*Synthesis*
Increase contract potential	Have skilled resource people	Financial risk if contracts are not won	Bid on contracts where resource persons are available
Spread firm philosophy	Demonstrate professional competence and expertise	Potential increased by contacts not by staff	Marketing equally important to contract gain
	Training can demonstrate management concern for employee development	Few firms have much philosophy to spread	Staffing can stimulate firm to putting values with image
	Create career path for qualified persons	Potential for career development rarely realized	Emphasis can be defined for management training and advancement
Use as base for diversifying activities	Can establish quick reputation	May exploit consulting for other purposes	Ensure multiple activities are well integrated

	Can set up and successfully test all "systems" within a firm	Other activities could cause demise of consulting function	Apply consulting widely to augment entire company's success
Sustain organizational structure	Large people base needed for pyramid organization	May be doing the right thing for wrong reasons and end up with large overhead expense	Need careful assessment of how organization structure affects hinng
	The more flexible the structure is. the more flexible the hiring policies can be	Structure can dictate hiring even when staffing is independent of organization design	Ensure structure that will not in hibit staffing level desired

teaming arrangements. Generally, firm managers who view people as being as important as the work will staff on an as-needed basis. Often, new firm members are brought in either to replace members who have left or to fill an opening created by a new contract. Flexible staffing policies (as shown in Exhibit 12-3) can increase the firm's service potential and provide greater training and growth for its employees.

There are any number of ways to define the positions in a consulting firm. Here are the most common types of professional staff:

Staff consultant. A person with minimal experience in consulting who comes to the firm in an entry-level position. Such a person has usually completed his or her education with a bachelor's degree, developed some technical or behavioral skill's in school, and might have had some previous short-term consulting experience. Such a person is likely to be promoted in one to three years.

Consultant. A person who has a bachelor's degree and an advanced degree in a specialty related to his or her consulting activities. This person is responsible for parts of projects and is actively seeking broader responsibilities. The person has written and oral communication skills.

This person will receive advanced level training and be ready for promotion in about one to three years.

Manager consultant. A person who is familiar with all aspects of consulting and has had significant experience in developing client/consultant relationships and completing assignments. This person manages a project from start to finish, participates in marketing activities, and assists in developing and implementing a strategic plan for the organization. This person functions as a principal-in-training and could be promoted to principal after completing the tasks outlined above. This person shares in the organization's marketing compensation and teaches consulting to other firm members.

Principal. This person is one of the leaders of the organization. His or her responsibilities include managing the firm, formulating policy, acquiring new engagements, and making final hiring decisions. Each client engagement has a principal-in-charge who assumes full responsibility for that assignment.

Administrative and staff support positions include office manager, financial director, editors, graphic artists, word-processing technicians, secretaries, and personnel/training administrators. Each person augments the consulting firm while contributing to the quality of the internal working environment. Exhibit 12-7 summarizes personnel in a consulting firm.

Sample Task II: Planning to Hire

1. Based on your firm's goals, its organization and staffing projections, develop a staffing plan.
   a. What are the elements in the plan?
   b. How will each one relate to each other?
   c. What provisions will be made for employee advancement, bonus plan, or special arrangements?
   d. Is the plan something each person must adhere to? Why?
   e. Will you end up with a personnel department? Describe the human resource concerns and functions that would follow from the plan.
2. Pick any two other plans. Relate the staffing plan to them. What are your findings?
3. When can you throw the plan away? Why?
4. What innovations are you willing to make in staffing your firm? What benefits can accrue from doing so? Can you justify whatever costs may be required?

RECRUITING AND SELECTING CANDIDATES

Increasing a consulting firm's staff **is** not unlike a client selecting a consultant. Just like a client, the consulting firm contacts or is contacted by potential consultants and decides who to hire based on the best presentation of

EXHIBIT 12-7

Levels of Consultant Responsibilities

Principal	Manager Consultant	Consultant	Staff Consultant	Support Staff
Provides leadership to firm operations and hires staff	Principal in training	Professional training and degree	Bachelor's or advanced degree	Provides expertise to common consulting functions
Completed many consulting assignments	Knowledgeable about all facets of consulting and successfully completed assignments	Basic knowledge of consulting business supplemented by advance training	New hire	Does not require previous consulting experience
Is responsible for marketing/execution of assignments in practice area	Has limited marketing and administrative responsibilities	Is privy to marketing calls and policy making meetings	Needs basic and advanced training	Are managerial, technical, or clerical personnel
Directly shares in firm profits	Limited profit sharing	Incentive is bonus	Incentive is increasing responsibility level	Career path is limited
Primary accruer of new projects	Manages consulting programs or multiple projects	Manages consulting project	Technical or behavioral researcher on specific project	Carry out most paperwork, accounting, or report production activities

credentials, personality, and potential. A firm should consider the following points in hiring staff:

Contact. A firm can contact a prospective employee in three ways: (1) directly, (2) through a recruiting agency, or (3) through unsolicited letters by the job seeker.

Screening. The assigned firm member or committee selects those candidates who meet the technical criteria (education and experience) for the position(s).

Interviewing. If interested in a prospective employee, the firm requests an interview. Generally, three or more staff members speak with the candidate. An interview format is presented in Exhibit 12-8. A candidate perspective is presented in Exhibit 12-9, describing a prepared, motivated, and shrewd potential firm member.

EXHIBIT 12-8

Consultant Action Sheet for Recruiting

Preparation
1. Determine job design for positions required, including:
   • Qualifications (experience, education, and special skills)
   • Responsibilities
   • Career advancement
   • Compensation and benefits
2. Advertise career opportunities through:
   • Word of mouth
   • Professional journals
   • Newspapers
   • Recruiting agencies
3. Screen resumes based on job design criteria.
4. Also, screen part-time, summer, or work/study employees for possible candidates.
5. Choose candidates and schedule interviews.
6. Decide on interview procedure and whether interviews conducted by individuals, group, or both.

Interview
1. Coordinate discussions to avoid repetition and to discover various aspects of candidate personality and abilities.
2. Help candidates feel "at home."

3. Develop a checklist for all information needed from candidate and how it will be obtained.
4. Allow candidate to initiate discussion.
5. Define evaluation method and use consistently for every interviewee.

Hiring
1. Determine leading candidates and talk further with each one. (Possibly schedule a second interview with top-level management as well as hiring manager.)
2. Gather and synthesize impressions from colleagues.
3. Check candidate's professional references.
4. Rank candidates and make decisions through consensus.

Either
5a. Make offer to candidate. Receive acceptance or make other offer. Finally, hire new firm member.
5b. Recruit further or cease activity.

EXHIBIT 12-9

Candidate Action Sheet for Recruiting

Preparation
1. Discover what career areas you want to enter or further.
2. Obtain information on potential consulting firms from:
   • Personal or professional contacts
   • Newspaper or journal advertisements
   • Reference books
   • Recruiting agencies
3. Decide on firms to contact.
4. Send credentials (in resume form plus cover letter) to chosen consulting firms.
5. Gather information about each firm that expresses interest in you.
6. Acknowledge and confirm interview time, place, and date.

Interview
1. Arrive on time and professionally dressed.
2. Open discussion by making statement about organization and asking a question about position.

3. Relate credentials to interviewer's answer, and ask another question about position.
4. Continue steps 2 and 3 until pertinent aspects of position and consulting environment are discovered, while relating your relevant experience and skills to interviewer.
5. Find out more about firm, including history, benefits, growth plans, and so forth.
6. Ask for feedback from interviewer(s).
7. Close interview cordially.
8. Carry out steps 2 through 7 for every interview.
9. Write follow-up letter if interested in position.

Negotiation
1. If an offer is not made, discover why—for future interviews.
2. If an offer is made, list pros and cons of becoming a member of consulting firm.
3. If not interested, write and respectfully decline.
4. If interested and need to negotiate compensation package, starting date, etc., schedule another meeting with primary contact.
5. Subsequent to the meeting, if you and the contact agree, then warmly accept.
6. If insufficient agreement occurs, respectfully decline in writing.

Testing. Some organizations ask their candidates to take cognitive and psychological tests to measure knowledge, attitudes, personality, interests, and motivation. The test results are both objective scores and subjective evaluations by the test administrator. Tests can convey useful information, but their importance should not be overrated.

Selection. Procedures and criteria used for selection can be as objective as a standardized test, or as biased as the founder's wishes. Most hiring decisions fall somewhere in between.

Decision. The firm makes an offer to the selected candidates. Since the benefits package and salary are primary to any prospective employee, a high-quality consulting firm will also entice a would-be consultant with such factors as:

- Well-defined career development paths.
- Autonomy, flexibility, and diversity in providing consulting services.

- Opportunities for client interaction and development of a client base.
- Desire for consultant's input to improve the firm's performance.

Sample Task III

Describe the profile for a Consulting Entrepreneur. What elements would it contain? What prerequisites are required? How would this entrepreneur differ from others?

Case Example 12-1: Ajax and the Lion

Ajax Consulting Engineers is beginning its annual recruitment drive. Harold Square is just about to look at the procedures for hiring candidates when the intercom rings. William Lion is on the other end.

W.L.: "Mr. Square, Will Lion here."

H.S.: "Yes, what can I do for you?"

W.L.: "I understand you are in the market for new employees."

H.S.: "How did you know? We haven't even begun our adver . . . ."

W.L.: "Oh, Mr. Square, from September 15 to October 15 Ajax hires new people like clock work."

H.S.: "Well, er--that's true, I suppose."

W.L.: "I understand your normal procedure is to post requirements in the trade journals and to consider only those applicants who fill out those notices."

H.S.: "Correct."

W.L.: "I would like then, sir, to directly suggest that, in my case, an exception be made due to my qualifications. They are head and shoulders above . . . ."

H.S.: "Mr. Lion, an exception for you is an exception for everyone. There will be no exceptions!"

W.L.: "You have put the same notice in the same trade journals for the past five years. How could this notice reflect your changing needs for people?"

H.S.: "I have examined more than 2000 people in my 18 years with Ajax, and 1 have never experienced belligerency like you are showing. Our procedures are set and we follow them, period, paragraph."

W.L.: "When can 1 make an appointment to see you?"

H.S.: "First fill out this year's notice. Then send it in with your resume, salary history, references, and a self-addressed, stamped envelope. We will contact you if further discussion is required."

W.L.: "What is clear is that rules are rules, period."
H.S.: "Precisely, what is clear is that rules are rules!"

ADVANCING THROUGH EDUCATION AND TRAINING

According to myth, consulting is an occupation that everyone practices but nobody really knows. This section attempts to dispel 1 that myth by presenting training programs for consultants and ways to evaluate performance. The techniques and tools required to carry out consulting engagements successfully are quite varied; however, the fundamental skills and attitudes remain the' same.

Education and training should begin from the professional's first day at the firm. There are two ways to orient a new employee: (1) intensive seminars or (2) selective discussions. In the first case, the employee participates alone or with other new employees in a one- or two-day briefing given by a senior manager. Topics discussed include the organization's history, structure, accounting methods, types of assignments, work methods, marketing strategies, and policies for compensation and advancement. The other method is for new employees to meet with the specific person -in charge of each of the departments listed above. For example, the comptroller discusses accounting and the personnel officer talks about benefits. Whichever method is used, the objectives remain the same-to acknowledge the new staff member, demonstrate a desire to have that person be a part of the organization, and offer a congenial, communicative environment. Exhibit 12-10 outlines a newcomer's first year.

Case Example 12-2: How Meaningful Is Tradition?

Peter Newcomer just joined Gilded, Inc., a prestigious management consulting firm located in Boston. The firm prides itself on "having the largest record of profit of any in our industry." On Peter's first day he was introduced to many of the Boston off ice professionals, and chatted briefly with the marketing principal, J. J. Push. A recent entrant into the consulting company, Helene Keen, volunteered to "show Peter the ropes."

Keen told Newcomer that he was to lunch with the founder, A. C. Proud. Tradition has it that during this lunch Mr. Proud conveys a secret or two of his success to the lucky beginner. "Not all new employees get this privilege," Helene was saying when the phone rang.

Proud's secretary is on the other end. "I'm sorry, Mr. Newcomer," she began, "but Mr. Proud will not be able to have lunch with you today." Peter was disappointed but did his other tasks to complete his first day. About two

---

EXHIBIT 12-10

Action Sheet for Acclimation of New Members

First Day
a. Greetings and welcome
  1. Visits with one or more principals
  2. Meets firm members
  3. Assigned a staff colleague to help with acclimation
b. Given information packet
  1. History of firm
  2. Operating philosophy
  3. Expected contributions
  4. Advancement guidelines
  5. Evaluation and review
  6. Training and job satisfaction
  7. Professional activities
  8. Summary
c. Completes benefits forms
  1. Fills out tax, insurance, and health forms
  2. Chooses benefits package
  3. Has health examination (optional)
  4. Has benefits counseling session

First Week
  a. Participates in company seminar
  b. Discovers area of responsibility
  c. Meets colleagues who will be working with and for

First Month
  a. Establishes professional relationship(s) with client(s)
  b. Develops rapport with consultants and management
  c. Produces first results on project
  d. Participates in training and other extracurricular activities

First Year
  a. Completes one or more consulting assignments
  b. Has one or more peer evaluation sessions
  c. Extends rapport with consulting colleagues
  d. Suggests and implements improvements to company operations
  e. Accomplishes one or more objectives toward career advancement
  f. Does one or more personal assessments about future with company

months later, Peter was hosting his third new hire. As with the other two new consultants, A. C. Proud took her out to lunch.

Peter is a strong but quiet person not easily upset by circumstances. Yet he started to wonder why he did not have lunch with the boss. Two months passed and Peter completed his first project. During his review session the principal nitpicks to a degree that Peter finds unwarranted. The colleagues involved are also surprised. Three months later, at his semiannual evaluation, Peter also receives flack for what he feels are minor errors. The next day he tries to make an appointment to see A. C. Proud, but his schedule is booked. At the end of the day the following Monday, Peter waits for Proud.

A. C. Proud appears on his way out. "Mr. Proud, may I have a word with you?" inquires Peter.

A.C.P.: "Who are you?"

P.N.: "Peter Newcomer."

A.C.P.: "Why do you wish to see me?"

P.N.: "Could we step inside your office for just a moment so I may explain?"

A.C.P.: "Yes, let us be brief."

Peter explained his tenure with Gilded, Inc., and his current worries about achievement and career advancement. Proud motioned Peter closer.

A.C.P.: "About seven years ago I personally managed a large contract for the U.S. Navy. The project officer was Peter Newcumber. Things went badly and we never completed the project. You say your name **is** Newcomer. I first heard it as Newcumber and that explains things. Word must have got around about the missed lunch and so the powers that be were not about to treat you any better than I had. Sometimes tradition can play nasty tricks on innocent people. I'll have the situation rectified."

During the orientation period, a new employee learns of the firm's philosophy regarding career development. Generally, career advancement is based on successful performance. If an employee does well and learns fast, so the theory goes, he will rise fast in the organization. Yet this principle is predicated on expansion and increased demand for services. Often, these conditions do not exist for long-enough periods to enable promotion. However, career advancement depends on the willingness of firm members to increase their levels of competency. Not everyone can become president; nevertheless, everyone can raise the quality of his work. Thus company leaders need to help firm members participate in a variety of consulting engagements. Exhibit 12-11 presents an overview of the abilities and skills consultants need to carry out engagements for clients (as derived from Chapter Six).

EXHIBIT 12-11

Consultant Competencies

Consulting Process Step	*Issue Abilities*	*Interpersonal Skills*
Need for change	N.A.*	N.A.*
Consultant selection	Understand client situation. Write proposal.	Develop client rapport. Assess compatibility with client.
Beginning engagement	Clarify contractual agreement. Identify chief client concerns.	Adapt to client situation.
Problem definition	Respect data confidentiality. Determine causes of problem. Collect and analyze data. Present information.	Build client trust. Build client communication channels. Use change strategies.
Resolution pathways	Develop decision framework. Outline implementation plan.	Use feedback. Be creative in designing solutions.
Pathway implementation	Create conflict resolution methods. Use implementation plan. Ensure budget not exceeded.	Build client independence. Build client comfort with changes. Confront client resistances.
Monitoring and termination	Write report. Present results. Finish project on time.	Provide quality assurance.
Evaluation and follow-up	Evaluate consultant. Evaluate client. Define ongoing tasks.	Give client feedback to consultant. Give consultant feedback to client.

_____

*Not applicable.

In-house training can foster these skills. Subjects for such sessions could include:

- Introduction to Consulting, a survey of the nature, purpose, and history of consulting, together with the types of consulting activities and an overview of the consulting process.
- The Consulting Process, an examination of the objectives, focus, and required abilities needed to carry out a successful consulting engagement.
- Communication Skills, a discussion of how to conduct a meeting, an interview, and a presentation; and how to write a proposal or a report.
- Professional Attitudes, an exploration of professional attitudes,

Topics for additional training sessions are listed in Exhibit 12-12.

Principals and managers of the firm also need to upgrade and develop their skills. Often, day-to-day pressures and responsibilities leave little time for

---

EXHIBIT 12-12

Additional Training Seminars

1. Communication Skills—Part II, a workshop focusing on means of establishing client rapport, being sensitive to client concerns, overcoming client resistance to change, and assisting in resolving client conflicts.
2. Planning a Consulting Assignment, a seminar directing the consultant on using planning methods to define and carry through a consulting engagement. Problem definition and decision-framing skills would be stressed.
3. Accounting, Contracts, and Proposals, a brief, intensive course on billings, fringe benefits, cost proposals, the in's and out's of administering a contract, and other topics of special interest.
4. Implementing and Evaluating a Consulting Assignment, a course showing how to formulate plans for resolving problems, monitor such plans, and evaluate the entire assignment. Case examples of both successful and not-so- successful consulting engagements will be given.
5. Marketing Made Straightforward, a seminar on how to develop a marketing plan, put it into effect, and modify it; how to establish contact with new clients; and how a consultant's efforts affect the rest of the organization.

continuing education. Yet the failure to broaden one's insights and improve one's abilities can prevent the firm from sustaining a competitive edge.

Within the firm, two means of giving feedback about areas for improvement are the self-assessment (Exhibit 12-13) and performance assessment.

Consultants perform two tasks that form the basis for reviews: they work on contracted projects and they contribute to the overall functioning of the

---

EXHIBIT 12-13

Self-Critique and Assessment

Name

Present position Years with firm

Current responsibilities:

Major achievements in the last year:

Major disappointments in the last year:

Factor	*Change*	*Hoped-for-change*
Authority		
Responsibility		
Satisfaction		
Career potential		
Growth in experience		
Interaction with clients		
Interaction with consultants		
Patience and tolerance		
Mental stimulation		
Contributions		

Main consulting strengths

Main consulting weaknesses:

Differences between this assessment and past one:

	Short Term	*Intermediate Term*	*Long Term*
Career aspirations			
Salary potential			
Career relationship to education			
Career relationship to family			
Career relationship to self-goals and professional growth			
Future in consulting			
Decision for consulting vocation Reasons			

Additional comments:

Immediate actions:

a.

b.

c.

d.

Date of assessment

Signature

organization. Exhibit 12-14 is a post-project evaluation, Exhibit 12-15 is a periodic overall review, and Exhibit 12-16 is feedback from the consultant to his evaluator.

Promotion policies within the firm need to be equitable; even more important, they need to be perceived as equitable. The directors of the firm want motivated, self-assured consultants who can tackle different client engagements, produce satisfying results for the client, and create market opportunities for the firm. The employee wants to apply his or her training

EXHIBIT 12-14

Evaluation of a Consulting Project

Name of employee _____

Position _____

Project title and code _____

Length of project _____

Description of project: _____

_____

_____

Consultant manager _____

Principal in charge _____

Employee's activities in project: _____

_____

_____

Amount of time spent on project _____

Evaluation Areas　　　　　　　　*Rating* Comments*

A. Consulting process

    1. Defined issue

    2. Found issue resolutions

    3. Assisted in choosing resolution pathways

    4. Developed pathway implementation

    5. Monitored implementation

    6. Evaluated assignment

    7. Performed within time and budget

B. Communications

    1. Proposal

    2. Internal memoranda

    3. Final report

4. Data collection

5. Presentation of findings

C. Client/staff rapport

    1. Addressed client concerns

    2. Achieved client commitment

    3. Identified ways for staff to improve skills

    4. Identified ways to improve consultant's skills

*1, excellent; 2, good; 3, satisfactory; 4, unsatisfactory.

Overall performance score _____

Suggestions for employee
improvement:

_____

_____

Employee's comments and
improvement suggestions:

_____

_____

Date of oral review

Signature of consultant manager _____

Signature of principal in charge. _____

EXHIBIT 12-15

Periodic Review of Consultants

Name of employee _____

Position _____

Principal conducting review _____

Evaluation Areas   *Overall Comments*

Consultant's strengths

Consultant's weaknesses

Consultant's improvement potential

Consultant's expected performance and why

Salary at last review

Benefits since last review

New total compensation

Potential contributions of consultant

Date of review

Signature of principal _____

Signature of employee _____

Employee comments: _____

EXHIBIT 12-16

Project Feedback

Name of employee _____
Position _____
Principal feedback receiving _____
Project manager receiving feedback _____
Evaluation Areas   *Rating Comments*

A. Preparation
   1. Received sufficient explanation and background
   2. Responsibilities were well defined
   3. Understood resource requirements and where to get them

B. Execution
   1. Received sufficient briefings throughout project
   2. Discussed problems as arose
   3. Solicited comments
   4. Critiqued contributions fairly
   5. Allowed to reach beyond prior responsibilities
   6. Principal/project manager devoted enough time to effort
   7. Principal/project manager able to correct mistakes

C. Competition _____
   1. Contributions to final report/presentation
   2. Efficient and pleasing use of consultant's time

3. Overall management performance
4. Project was learning experience
5. Would work again with principal or project manager
1, excellent; 2, good; 3, satisfactory; 4, unsatisfactory.
Overall performance score

Suggestions for principal/project manager improvement:

_____

Principal/project manager comments and improvement suggestions:

_____

_____

Date of feedback _____
Signature of employee _____

and experience to different client environments in order to improve his or her abilities, reputation, and finances. When aspirations and performance do not match, consultant and principal need to reassess the consultant's future with the firm. Both parties need to be frank and mature in this exchange. If an employee is terminated, every effort should be made to assist in his or her relocation. If, on the other hand, the consultant voluntarily terminates employment, effort should be made to find out the underlying reasons for this decision.

Sample Task V

For each of the following actions write a brief situation where it occurred or could occur. A firm member:

- Is fired
- Is laid off
- Is terminated
- Is relieved of responsibilities
- Quits
- Takes a leave of absence
- Resigns voluntarily
- Asks for a transfer

Which situations could the firm have prevented? How? Which situations could the firm do nothing about? Why? What are the implications for the firm's hiring policies, training activities, types of consulting services provided, or the attitudes of the principals?

Case Example 12-3: Symbol as Policy

Date: January 29, 1983
To: Lawrence Lendler, Principal
From: jack junior
Subject: Grounds for Dismissal

This memo is written as a reflection of the past few weeks' activities that have led you to request my resignation. Last July, guidelines were issued on "career advancement" within the firm, specifying what achievements need be done to "move up the ladder." Basically, there now is a three-tiered system in which an entry-level member can become a principal. The memo was greeted with approval, as it provided incentives to work to a higher level. These guidelines not only specified the accomplishments needed for higher status and salary, but also the responsibilities required in that level. It is clear that as one person acquires more control and influence over the affairs of the company, he or she will also impart direction to the company, in part, through the business contracts procured.

This is one of the implicit responsibilities of being an executive.

However, the directive of last July is a set of guidelines. That is, aspiring consultants are to, whenever possible, adhere to this activity plan in order to advance. Should it be held to exclusively? Are there no other conditions for promotion?

And what are the underlying motivations of management in ensuring the directive? In November, these questions were indirectly asked and answered. As you know, I was working with a government client in developing a management information scheme for his planning responsibilities. The project was about over, and I learned of a need for follow-on consulting assistance. My colleague Perry Perrington and I put together a short presentation showing how our firm could give such assistance. We made this presentation to the client. The client was impressed and said he would like us either to assist in writing the competitive procurement or to bid on the procurement. We were excited. The positive and professional rapport we had been developing with the client looked like it was going to pay off in spades.

However, this sequence of events was mostly a no-no according to the "higher-ups." When you found out what we did, your reactions were less than positive. In fact, your concern was whether our action could, in any way, endanger the security of your personal marketing activities, or possibly undermine the reputation (spelled "image") of the firm. Thus you immediately called a halt to this out-of-sequence activity, and subsequently urged me to resign. I would not, and now I am about to be fired.

It is clear that you are hurt, Mr. Lendler, because I so thoughtlessly tried to usurp your authority. Never mind that the activity is an extension of previous client work. Never mind the fact that the client had not been receptive to your attempts at business development. Further, no contract was signed, all discussions were general, and a formal proposal was not submitted. But the conversation, nonetheless, is enough to anger you.

Whether I stay or go is not the issue. The issue is the use of guidelines as rules to let us know what we can and cannot do. The advancement system is more a way of keeping people in well-defined nooks then of allowing or pushing for individual growth and contribution. What is said between the lines is as follows:

- Thou shalt follow the guidelines to the letter.
- Thou shalt not perform responsibilities of another position lest one be fired.
- Thou shalt uphold and sustain the power of those in charge.
- Marketing is a right given by advancement to the inner sanctum, not a privilege earned through initiative and contribution.

I hereby designate this communiqué to be my acceptance of your dismissal. A company that runs more on taboos than opportunities is not my kind of firm.

KNOWING HOW TO CONTROL

Control simply means measuring the firm's performance by defining measures for evaluating projects or assessing potential contract work. In either case, a controlling procedure includes the following points:

1. Define standards of performance.
2. Measure actual performance.
3. Compare actual performance with planned performance.
4. Evaluate deviations.
5. Determine the appropriate actions to correct any deviations.

Control should operate as a system and function in the following manner: To keep track of a project's cash flow, the project manager periodically enters all costs incurred in the project. These costs are labor and material expenses plus the overhead charge for executing the contract based on the firm's overhead rate. (Remember, the overhead rate is the overhead costs divided by direct labor expenditures. See Chapter Eight.)

The manager then receives a printout of the work to date showing the differences between actual and planned costs. Expended and unexpended dollars by expense category are shown. The planned project budget is the average periodic costs over the life of the contract based on the client payment schedule.

The defined standards for a project budget (beside the overhead rate) include the direct labor cost, material expenses, and profit in terms of a percentage of the revenue from the contract. These percentages are used to assess budget deviations and attempt to correct them. Correcting situations where project cash flow becomes negative is not immediate. Errors of assignment: of expenditures, appropriation of project revenues for other activities, above-normal material expenses, and so on, could cause money losses. Turning around the method of project spending could be done by correcting computer errors, reallocating lost funds, and watching over charges for labor, report production, and other expense items. Devices to accomplish this turn around include the weekly work log (Exhibit 6-7) and direct expense control sheet (Exhibit 8-13), as well as summaries of expenditures by each employee for each contract billed and total expenditures for each contract by all employees in the format of Exhibits 8-12 and 8-14.

When the project is complete, a final budget statement is produced (Exhibit 12-17). This sheet lists a breakdown of revenues spent, total costs, and profit for the project. The pattern of expenditures is scrutinized to discern how any management mistakes can be eliminated in the future. Exercising control over a project is important because small errors in judgment can lead to large wastes of funds. For example, Exhibit 12-18 shows a sensitivity analysis for some cost factors, and demonstrates the need to use the aforementioned control procedure to prevent cost overruns.

The control procedure can project future revenues for potential contracts. This forecasting task entails two items: contract negotiation and contract opportunities. By applying standards of financial risk (see Chapter Ten) to a given contract and comparing them to the payment scheme, a decision can be made to bid on the contract.

Backlog is the term applied to total contract opportunities. Contract backlog consists of awards and leads. Awards are the contracts the firm has accrued but not yet performed. Leads are the projected services the firm expects to procure. Award backlog is plotted monthly for all in-house contracts. It is compared to total expenses for all project and aggregate profit to ascertain the solvency level of the firm.

Also, contract backlog is compared to the firm's capacity limit (that is, the maximum revenue that could be generated by a given staff size). Trends are noted and stated in the quarterly and annual report, together with how well contract targets were met and how contract issues were resolved. The purpose of

EXHIBIT 12-17

Sample Project Budget Sheet

Project title   *Contract code*

Contract No.   Type of contract

Client

Start date   End date

Budget item   Amount

1. Revenues

2. Direct labor

3. Overhead (% of item 2)

4. Administration (% of items 2 + 3) _____

5. Direct expenses

6. Total costs _____

7. Profit (% of items 2 + 3 + 4)

                                          Month

Projection Summary	*May*	*June*	*July*	*Aug.*	*Sept.*	*Oct.*
Projected revenue						
Actual revenue						
Project costs						
Actual costs						
Percent completion						
Prepared by, Project Manager						

* By method of award: cost plus fixed fee, firm fixed price, time and materials, or other.

keeping records and doing projections is to be more responsive to the changing nature of the firm's financial picture.

MEASURING A FIRM'S PERFORMANCE

One way to sustain the viability of a firm is to critique it periodically. For example, to assess a firm's staffing the measures to be evaluated would first be defined (as stated in Exhibit 12-19); then the measure of interest would

EXHIBIT 12-18

Effects of Cost Variations*

Item	Reference Case	Case 1	Case 2	Case 3
1. Revenues	$4,000	$4,000	$4,000	$4,000
2. Direct labor	1,000	1,050	1,100	1,000
3. Overhead (70% of item 2)	700	735	770	700
4. Subtotal (items 2 + 3)	1,700	1,785	1,870	1,700
5. Administration (37% of item 4)	629	660.45	691.90	629
6. Subtotal (items 4 + 5)	2,329	2,445.45	2,561.90	2,329
7. Direct expenses	1,200	1,200	1,200	1,320
8. Total costs (items 6 + 7)	3,529	3,645.45	3,761.90	3,649
9. Net revenue (item 1-tem 8)	471	364.55	238.10	351

* Using Exhibit 8-5. Case 1 is a 5% increase in direct labor resulting in a 22.6% decrease in net revenue. Case 2 is a 10% increase in direct labor resulting in a 49.4% decrease in net revenue. Case 3 is a 10% increase in expenses resulting in a 25.4% decrease in net revenue.

EXHIBIT 12-19

Measures of Personnel Activities

General	Project	Evaluation
Salary levels	Marketing	Changes recognized
Membership growth	Proposal writing	Changes begun

Membership turnover	Project management	Changes implemented
Membership advancement	Project support	
Membership age distribution		
Membership experience		
Membership educational level		
Training of members		
Extracurricular activities		
Membership benefits		
Vacation/sick leave		
Changes in overhead, etc.		

be chosen; the data collected and examined for trends, disparities, and commonalities; the conclusions considered for firm policies; and then suggestions would be made to implement these changes. In Exhibit 12-20, salary levels are critiqued to ascertain if they reflect changes to clients and if they are competitive with other firms. The findings are somewhat surprising. First, not only is it true that the higher the position in the firm, the more absolute dollars will be made, but also the faster such earnings will increase. This observation implies that client billings are heavily weighted toward principal and manager consultants. That is, given normal yearly contracts, principals and managers will earn their annual salary with fewer contracts than staff consultants. Further, there is evidence suggesting that consultants and managers are slightly underpaid, principals are a bit overpaid, and staff consultants are definitely underpaid.

If staff consultant salaries are to be raised to a competitive range, the rate for principals needs to be lowered to maintain current billing rates.

Pressure is put on management to make use of the guidelines of Exhibit 12–20. Thus, if a decision is made to modify the salary scale, notice should be given to the entire membership. Also, the scheme for making and monitoring all subsequent changes that may be required to the client billing scale must be noted and reported in subsequent newsletters or periodic status reports.

The second example presents a different side to the situation. Exhibit **12-21** displays the figures for new hires, promotions, and departures. In perusing this chart, one questions how close these shifts are to the norm.

EXHIBIT 12-20
Example 1: Are Salaries Commensurate and Competitive?

Indicator	Principal	Manager Consultant	Consultant	Staff Consultant
1. Raw data				
a. Current	$64,000–50,000	$48,000–40,000	$38,000–31,000	$29,000–20,000
b. Percent increase per year	28%	20%	18%	12%
2. Commensurate data				
a. Billing for person/year	$100,000	$80,000	$60,000	$40,000
b. Percent of billing which is salary	40%	30%	25%	20%
3. Competitive data				
a. Current annual level	$60,000–54,000	$54,000–40,000	$40,000–32,000	$32,000–24,000
b. Percent increase per year	25%	22%	20%	25%

*Available in consulting association reports on compensation. Specifically, the Association of Consulting Management Engineers has such documents.

EXHIBIT 12-21

Example 2: Are Members on the Run?

Indicator	Principal Consultant	Manager Consultant	Consultant	Staff Consultant	Technical Support	Clerical
1. Employment turnover						
a. 1984 departures	0	2	6	10	2	5
b. Percent of staff	*	25%	30%	20%	20%	25%
c. Departed employed 1 year or less	—	1	4	7	1	3
d. 1983 departures	1	0	4	8	1	4
2. Employment advancement						
a. Number of promotions, 1984	1	0	1	2	1	
b. Time in position before promotion (years)	2	—	3	3	2V2	
c. Number of promotions, 1983	2	3	1	0	1	—
3. Employment growth						
a. Number of new hires, 1984	0	1	3	4	1	4
b. Total staff	5	7	18	46	10	19
c. Number of new hires, 1983	1	0	0	2	2	3

*A dash means not applicable.

Studies or no studies, it is wrong to fit a particular firm's employment pattern into a normal curve. Instead, what one can do is ask what effect industry trends are having on the firm. Referring to Exhibit 12-20, we saw that staff consultants were being underpaid, which could explain why the turnover rate has increased in the last two years. Further, it is clear that there will always be a nonzero level of attrition, due to better offers, career change, illness, and other factors. This observation probably explains the turnover in clerical personnel and, to a lesser extent, the other positions as well.

Still, the large turnover in the consultant staff consultant categories suggests that other factors should be considered. For example, most of the staff left within one year of being hired, which could signal a closer scrutiny of the hiring procedures and training given to new firm members. In fact, the outcome of such an inquiry could lead to changes in firm policy concerning new hires, promotion, career development, and other incentives.

The third example focuses on quantifying consulting activities outside contract work. Exhibit 12-22 shows three types of activities. Too many of

---

EXHIBIT 12-22
Example 3: Is Time Being Misspent?

Indicator	Principal	Manager Consultant	Consultant	Staff Consultant
1. Proposal writing				
a. Percent time per month (avg.), 1984	10	20	30	15
b. Percent of staff per	80	60	100	70
c. Percent time per month (avg.), 1983	12	18	30	10
2. Marketing				
a. Percent time per month (avg.), 1984	70	40	15	15

b. Percent of staff per month (avg.)	100	80	30	5
c. Percent time per month (avg.), 1983	65	45	20	5
3. Extracurricular				
a. Percent time per month (avg.), 1984	5	20	25	10
b. Percent of staff	3–5	10	10–12	3–5
c. Percent time per month (avg.), 1983	5	12	15	10

the staff or too much time is being spent on the proposal activity above the targeted level. Knowing this, changes could be proposed in the way proposals are generated. Also, more emphasis could be placed on the extracurricular involvement encouraging more "play" for better work.

ESTABLISHING FORMAL OPERATING PROCEDURES

One of the basic consequences of a consulting firm's "evolution" is the creation of policy and structured communication channels. They can be as elaborate *or* as simple as the members' actions dictate, but they are to assist in reviewing and strengthening the firm's operations. Exhibit 12-3 is an example of a staffing policy statement. Based on this statement, procedures for recruitment, acclimation, career evaluation, and advancement are developed. Similarly, marketing and controlling policies lead to the development of those department's functions.

The corporate report illustrated in Exhibit 12-23 is the mainstay for reviewing firm functions on a periodic basis. Each major firm function organizing, staffing, marketing, controlling, and consulting-is studied. The purpose of these reports is to assess the state of each function, present any issues or concerns, and discuss potential ways to handle them.

EXHIBIT 12-23
Documents Required to Operate a Consulting Firm

Documents

Planning	Organizing	Staffing	Controlling
Firm charter	Organizational form/content	Hiring, acclimating, and advancement policies	Billing methods Taxes
Firm bylaws	Procedures for policy formulation, decision making, and communication	Evaluation procedures	Revenue analysis
Strategic plan		Performance measurement	Cost-efficiency improvements
Marketing plan	Mechanisms for coping with change		

Period

Weekly	Monthly	Quarterly	Annually
Marketing report Staff news	Marketing report Evaluation reports	Marketing report Advancement news	Marketing report Modified strategic plan or marketing plan
		New organizational arrangements	
Policy/procedural changes	Committee reports on various firm aspects	Financial review and critique	Financial evaluation and projection

CONSIDERING DIVERSIFICATION

The word "diversify" usually connotes a smorgasbord of services, yet there are other ways to diversify. This section briefly describes three such avenues: (1) service, (2) location, and (3) corporate structure. These paths are not mutually exclusive and can occur at *the* same time. In any case, the main reason for diversifying is the same: to enable the firm to reduce the boom-and-bust cycle of client work.

Service Expansion. Here the consulting firm ventures into new fields, services, and/or ways to provide them. Increasing the number of services is a function of:

- Prior successes with existing services.
- The willingness of firm members to harness new resources.
- The ability of the organization to handle new services.

Generally, a doctor, lawyer, or accountant concentrates his practice in one or two well-defined areas. Consulting tends to provide a broader array of services because of the client's changing organization and the consultant's desire for a wider array of experiences. Yet to provide these additional services well, the consulting firm's policymaking, staffing, marketing, controlling, and consulting functions must be able to absorb the new services.

Sample Task V

Assume that you **are** an owner of a 15-person consulting firm specializing in testing the strength of various metals. Your clients have been satisfied with your work. Now you and the other firm members want to add a computer analysis package with the service. How will this affect new sales, repeat business, or client satisfaction? How will this affect the marketing, consulting, and staffing methods of the firm?

Geographic spread. The decision to open more than one office is based on the following goals:

- To serve existing clients more effectively.
- To enlarge the firm's image.
- To have a marketing presence for future contacts and contracts.
- To provide services in a cost-effective manner to many similar clients at the same time.

Again, new offices are not opened until, like the first off ice, there is enough business to support them. But having the workings of the firm in place shortens the startup time of subsequent offices. Another facet of multiple offices is communication. If the first office acts as "home," then all other offices are "field" and take their cues from the home office. But the nature of services, types of clients, and style of management would probably differ from office to office. Thus flexibility in the communication network is key to incorporating interoffice differences and allowing new ideas, policies, and techniques to arise from any office. On the other hand, similarities in operating philosophy, consulting procedure, and management practices will exist in every office, reflecting a uniform impression of the firm.

An offshoot of having multiple offices would be to provide consulting methods via a franchise arrangement: that is, to market consulting services to prospective consultants who would pay a fee for learning and using the reputable procedures of the franchiser. These consultants would then open offices and build their own clientele based on offering the franchised services. A consulting franchiser called General Business Services of Rockville, Maryland, has done this. Such an arrangement is appealing since many consultants have an entrepreneurial spirit. Therefore, multiple services with multiple offices implies a consulting organization that shares a common philosophy, operating methods, and encourages initiative and creativity in handling client concerns.

Corporate structure. A small consulting firm can share operations or merge with another small firm (as discussed in Chapter Three). Also, it can become part of a larger corporation as a subsidiary or as an internal consulting unit. A nonservice company or a service conglomerate would offer to purchase the consulting operations as a subsidiary because:

- There is a potential high return on investment.
- The reputation or image of the company would be enhanced.
- Assistance could be given in marketing other services.
- Advice could be transferred to many areas in the company.

In most arrangements of this sort, the buyer assumes the liabilities of the consulting firm. In return, corporate policies are followed by the seller.

Further, the consulting firm owners or all members receive not only an inducement to sell but also a cash bonus, stock options, board membership, and autonomy. In most cases, the consulting firm remains self-governing, with only minor changes in its operating methods. The owners (sellers) will continue to manage the firm and will receive payments for joining the buyer's "fold." As a profit center, a portion of the consulting firm's profits will go to corporate headquarters as well as taking on its accounting structure. In return, the firm will generally have access to the facilities, expertise, or support systems of the other subsidiaries.

Or the buying company can use the consulting firm as its own internal consulting unit. However, with this arrangement, the parent company would take a more active part in determining the consulting functions, including:

- Are there enough existing or potential issue areas within the organization to warrant having a full-time consulting group?
- Can the functional unit engender a sense of objectivity, neutrality, and respect in the consultants' work?
- Will a procedure be in place for selecting the internal consultant's staff?
- What opportunities will exist for internal consultants to broaden their development and advance their careers?
- How will external consultants be used and relate to internal consultants?
- It has been observed that large corporations are prime users of internal consulting groups.

Acceptance by professional staff (at all levels in both buyer and seller organizations) of internal consulting is the key to high performance. This acceptance is predicated on establishing career advancement and incentive programs that will provide security to the internal practitioners, while encouraging objective, creative, and interactive consulting. Further, allowing the internal consultants to be the "managers" of external consultants can motivate both parties to learn from each other. Exhibit 12-24 presents distinctions

---

EXHIBIT 12-24

Characteristics of External and Internal Consultants

External	*Internal*
1. Provides consulting services based on working with other organizations on similar assignments.	1. Provides consulting services based on working with other departments (of the organization) on similar tasks.
2. Function in organization is to be an objective, short-term investigator/facilitator of client issue definition and resolution	2. Function in organization is to be an influential, ongoing presence in handling long-term assignments.
3. Responsibility is to handle client issue with independent, outside perspective.	3. Responsibility is to handle client issue with a compromising perspective.

4. Authority is to client alone (considering objectives of organization).

4. Authority is to client, superiors, and top administrators.

5. Reward is issue-resolved, using effective judgments and techniques to accomplish it.

5. Reward is issue resolved using trade-offs between influence and career advancement in organization.

6. Decide on consulting assignments based on preference.

6. Decide on consulting assignments based on organizational pressures.

7. Inadequate internal staff or large internal backlog are motivators for seeking services.

7. Need for efficient and effective use of all organizational resources is motivation for seeking services.

8. Projects tend to be on an as-needed basis, focused around policy, organizational structure and functions, recurring issues, or specialized concerns.

8. Projects tend to be long term, focused on management surveys, systems procedures, and long-run planning.

9. Can work alone, or in teams.

9. Generally work in teams.

10. Tend to use services for new technology, policy, technique, or implementation or feasibility study.

10. Tend to use services where proprietory information is involved.

between the two. Internal consultants would generally work on confidential issues. External consultants would be called in for projects of short duration in which either the skills or experience of the internal group have been inadequate. Such outside consultants would perform the needed consulting and in so doing transfer the knowledge and insight gained to the internal group, who, in turn, would provide all data and organization information requested. Working together, useful assistance can be given to rectifying organizational issues.

Whatever means are used to broaden the consulting activities; they must be carried out with good management. The elements stressed previously-a perceptive sense of organization and knowledge of policymaking, a sensitivity to firm members' needs, and insightful consulting directions-are the rudiments of both short- and long-term owners. For these reasons, be leery of either acquiring or being merged with a business whose management does not understand these elements.

Sample Task VI

What are the factors that determine how fast a firm grows? What are the consequences if it grows too slow, or too fast? Can one find an optimal rate of growth? How would it be done?

SUMMARY AND EXTENSION

This chapter has tackled the major decision of consulting growth-whether or not to start a firm. At the outset, Exhibit 12-1 showed two different attitudes toward forming a firm. One is the desire to sustain and upgrade the consulting practice without encumbering it within an organizational framework. The other attitude expressed the desire to build a broader consulting influence and scale of assignments that required the support and resources of a firm. As the chapter continued, it became clearer that the two attitudes were really not disparate. In his "mind" the solo practitioner has the image, direction, and abilities to achieve a successful consulting practice. The consulting firm is merely the articulation of these mental insights in an organizational design. The attitudes encompass the will to perform consulting services productively for the mutual enrichment of client and consultant. This concept in the short term, and more in the long term, characterizes a satisfying consulting environment.

Productivity is a measure of how effectively a set amount of output results from a stated amount of input. In consulting, the major inputs are capital and know-how. The major outputs are consulting assignments. The better the firm is equipped to improve the skills and motivation of its members, the higher the productivity. Therefore, the challenge of the individual consultant turned consultant manager is to (in concert with all other firm members) achieve an operational consensus which brings results and contentment. As the next chapter will show, accomplishing this aim has ramifications beyond the firm, the consulting services, or the clients. For such a firm can be an example of the future-an example of consulting as a key agent of change in society.

Chapter Thirteen

Looking Ahead

SNAPSHOT

Having completed our detailed look at consulting, the-last step is to look at what lies ahead for consultants. In this chapter we describe ways to cope with the changing nature of a consultancy.

INSTITUTING CHANGE IN YOUR CONSULTING PRACTICE

Today, there are more individual consultants and consulting firms than ever before. All major indicators confirm this point.

- The U.S. Census of Service Industries counts a 50 percent increase in management consultancies over the last census and a 94 percent increase in annual sales. Furthermore, 80 percent of these firms employed fewer than 10 people, and 75 percent of the consultancies are corporations.
- Consultants and consulting organizations have had a steadily increasing membership.
- The biennial Business Practices Survey in Consulting Engineer magazine showed an increase in consulting engineering firms.
- Since 1977 six new consulting associations have formed in the United States.

It is clear that consultants and consulting are playing an increasing rote in the affairs of business, government, and society. However, on the qualitative

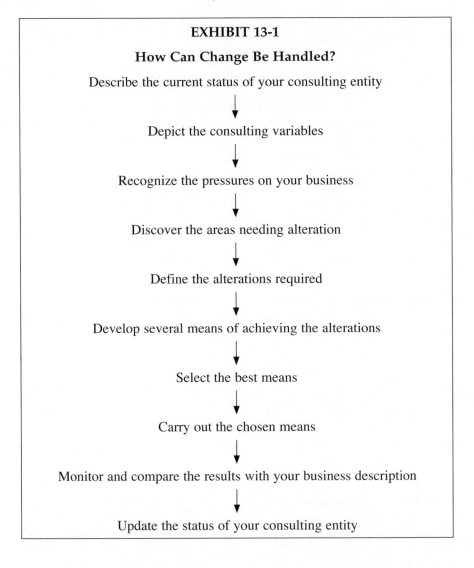

EXHIBIT 13-1

How Can Change Be Handled?

Describe the current status of your consulting entity

Depict the consulting variables

Recognize the pressures on your business

Discover the areas needing alteration

Define the alterations required

Develop several means of achieving the alterations

Select the best means

Carry out the chosen means

Monitor and compare the results with your business description

Update the status of your consulting entity

side, how well are consultants providing services, developing their practices, and responding to changing influences?

To answer these questions we must examine how effectively consultants cope with change. And this chapter presents a method for systematically, comprehensively, and dynamically preparing and adapting to change.

Exhibit 13-1 presents a chart on how change can be handled. The first step is to sit down and take stock of your practice-what ails it and what stimulates it? Then ask yourself how you can incorporate the needed changes so that your consultancy remains viable, competitive, and satisfying.

Sample Task I

Carry out the method described in Exhibit 13-1 for your consulting practice. What strengths do you find? What areas for improvement do you discover? How will your improvement increase your strengths? What approach will you use to implement such improvements? How often will you review your business progress? Why?

Four different types of consulting organizations are described in Exhibit 13-2. You can describe your own firm by simply and straightforwardly stating what your consultancy is, who the clients are, what services you provide, where you practice, and what, if any, your future plans are.

(Note: This depiction combines the descriptions noted in Chapters Three and Four.)

EXHIBIT 13-2

Examples of Consulting Entities

1. Freelance. A one-person operation that provides technical assistance to small firms. Specifically, the service is a planning system to recapture waste resources from leather tanneries. The clients are located in New England and the Midwest. The consultant meets with operations personnel on a retainer/profit basis. Future plans call for consulting with foreign tanners.

2. Trainer. A one-person operation that works on organizational development as an internal consultant at a medium-size hospital. The consultant's mission is to upgrade the working environment for all personnel. The projects last a long time, with follow-up activities. The clients tend to be small groups from one or more divisions. The learning consists of conflict resolution, improving communication skills, and ways to participate in policymaking and implementation.

3. Generalist. A multiperson operation that works on finding new budgeting techniques and resolving financial problems with state and county government budgeting offices. In addition, the financial personnel usually participate in training seminars given by the

consultants. The firm is organized by projects with employees being grouped by academic skills, so various employees can be working on several projects at the same time. The projects encompass one or more stages of the consulting process. The firm is an autonomous part of a conglomerate.

4. Auxiliary. A multiperson operation that is part of a large electronics company. The division specializes in quality assurance and testing of the firm's new products. The services are used to define the product specifications and examine the resultant hardware. The division's members can perform quality assurance for any phase of product development. The major "client" using the consulting is the vice-president of marketing. *The firm is* considering providing external consulting to other electronics producers.

Next, use Exhibit 13-3 to note the primary features of your practice. (This is done in Exhibit 13-4.) Then contemplate and write out the pressures facing your business now. What external forces affect your consultancy? What internal actions reduce the strength of the practice? Exhibit 13-5 lists some general factors to ponder. Specific pressures can be deduced from these generalizations, illustrated in Exhibit 13-6. If you follow the example through the remaining viewgraphs, you will see what alterations are required to keep the consultancy vibrant and how each alteration can be achieved (Exhibit 13-7). The remaining activities are carried out by making and implementing a decision.

First, take the alterations listed in Exhibit 13-7 and rank your alterations (using Exhibit 13-1. Then decide which alternatives will be used based on the decision criteria of Exhibit 13-8. The example shown in Exhibit 13-9 demonstrates that the alternatives are all useful; it is a matter of resources, management, cost, or time limitations. That is, eventually all alternatives should be enacted,

Finally, detail the actions required to implement the alternatives. Monitor the impacts of implementation and make minor corrections as needed. The bottom line is to strengthen the consultancy's business posture for the present and the future. Yet, a stronger consulting practice means both smart business actions and a high level of motivation. As mentioned in Chapter One, a balance must be found between attitude, activities, and actions so that the consultant can grow with the business. This balance represents the true, long-term health of your practice. Are you ready to achieve success?

EXHIBIT 13-3

Characteristics of the Consulting Field

Type of Consultant
External
Internal

Single
Institute
Firm

Type of Services
Technical
Behavioral
Combination

Range of Services
Specific
Semigeneral
General

Consulting Process Usage
One stage
Multiple stages
All stages

Consulting Organizational Structure
Single
Group
Division

Matrix
Pyramid
Practice centers

Types of Clients per Assignment
Individual
Group
Intergroup
Mixed

Consulting Assignments

Contracts
One-time
Extended
Mixed

Time Frame
Short-term
Medium-term
Long-term

Dollar Amount
Small-scale
Medium-scale
Large-scale

Type of Client Organization

Size	Sector	Type of Office
Small	Private	Domestic
Medium	Public	Foreign
Large	Institutional	

Income Status	Size
Profit	Large
Nonprofit	Medium
	Small

Type of External Consulting Firm

Ownership	Corporate Status
Sole proprietorship	Stand alone
Partnership	Part of a conglomerate
Privately held corporation	Franchise
Publicly held corporation	
Hybrid (institute, consortium, etc.)	

External Consulting Locations

Kind of Office	Coverage
Main	Nationwide
Branch	Regionwide

EXHIBIT 13-4

Examples of Consulting Entities*

Characteristics

Entity	Consultant Type	Service Type	Service Range	Organization Structure	Process Use	Consulting Assignments	Client Type	Client Organization Type	External Consulting Locations	External Consulting Firm Type
Free lance	External/ individual	Technical	Specific	N.A.*	One stage	Short-term, small-scale, unique	Group	Small, private	Domestic main, office, regionwide	Small, profit, stand alone, sole proprietor ship
Trainer	Internal/ individual	Behavioral	Semigeneral	N.A.	All stages	Long-term medium scale. ongoing	Mixed	Medium, in stitutional	N.A.	N.A.
Generalist	External/ firm	Combination	General	Matrix	Mul- tiple stages	Medium- term, medium scale mixed	Mixed	Medium, public	Domestic, statewide	Medium, profit. part of conglomerate, privately held corporation
Auxiliary	Internal/ division	Technical	Specific	Practice centers	Mul- tiple stages	Short-term, large scale. unique	Indi- vidual	Large, private	N.A.	N.A.

*N.A., not applicable.

EXHIBIT 13-5

Consulting Business Pressures

External	*Internal*
Client's industry trends	Management
Specific clients' problems	Performance
Other consultants' activities	Purpose of consultancy
Association developments	Personal
Variance in laws and regulations	
Economic constraints	

EXHIBIT 13-6

**Sensing Pressures on Consultancy and Finding
Business Areas Requiring Responses**

External Pressures
1. Competition for consulting has dramatically increased.
2. Clients' procurement processes are cumbersome and political.
3. State legislation to limit consulting services.
4. The clients have shown a surplus in the last two years.

Internal Pressures
1. Developing financial consulting products.
2. Decline in marketing efforts.
3. Owner considering selling firm and becoming independent again.
4. Experiencing high staff turnover.

Responses
1. Firm definition.
2. Client mix.
3. Type of services provided.
4. Type of assignments.

EXHIBIT 13-7

Alterations Required and Means to Achieve Them

Redefine the Firm
1. Institute participatory management.
2. Develop matrix organization.
3. Expand client base and consulting services with conglomerate.
4. Increase service sales by 70 percent over next 18 months.

Rethink Mix of Clients
1. Provide existing clients with broader range of services.
2. Provide new clients with existing services.
3. Market to clients in other geographic areas.

Broaden Types of Services
1. Develop consulting products.
2. Define expanded set of services.
3. Specify practice areas and their directors.
4. Fill expertise voids for new services.

Reassess Assignments
1. Increase variety of consulting contracts (i.e., short term, long-term, one-time, or follow-on); small or large revenue.
2. Publicize expanded services and how they are offered.
3. Encourage project management and client contact.
4. Improve consulting process to have specified ways of defining client problem and establishing client rapport.

EXHIBIT 13-8

Ranking and Choosing the Alternatives

Rank the alterations by:
    a. Sequence of events to be done
    b. immediate importance
    c. Risk

Choose among the alternatives in each alteration using:
a. Primary decision criteria
    1. Time to implement
    2. Cost of implementation
    3. Availability of resources
b. Secondary decision criteria
    1. Compatibility with consultancy's purpose
    2. Degree to which alternative can be tried on a limited basis first
    3. Level of resistance to change

EXHIBIT 13-9

Example of Ranking and Choosing

Rank the Alterations
1. Redefining the firm is foremost since all else follows from this.
2. Reassessing assignments has the most immediate impact on level of business.
3. Rethinking mix of clients—takes longer to do than reassessing assignment, but it should be done.
4. Broadening types of services has the most risk of the four areas.

Choose Among the Alternatives in Each Alteration Area
1. Getting more people involved in management can help reduce the costs of increasing business volume inside and outside the conglomerate.
2. Publicity seems the quickest, easiest, but costliest alternative. Thus reduce overhead by disseminating capabilities statement to all current clients. Improve the consulting process services and use this to broaden the variety of contract work.
3. Set targets for contacting clients, presenting services, and achieving new business. Would do this for existing clients first, then new clients. New geographic areas are too costly to penetrate at this time.
4. Redefine my services. Put hold on products until I can afford to develop them. Specifying practice areas is counter to more open management. Increasing the staff meets a lot of resistance. Find ways to overcome this resistance.

Index